Y0-BQO-996

MYSTERIES, LEGENDS, AND UNEXPLAINED PHENOMENA

LAKE AND SEA MONSTERS

MYSTERIES, LEGENDS, AND UNEXPLAINED PHENOMENA

Astrology and Divination

Bigfoot, Yeti, and Other Ape-Men

ESP, Psychokinesis, and Psychics

Ghosts and Haunted Places

Lake and Sea Monsters

Shamanism

UFOs and Aliens

Vampires

Werewolves

Witches and Wiccans

MYSTERIES, LEGENDS, AND UNEXPLAINED PHENOMENA

LAKE AND SEA MONSTERS

LINDA S. GODFREY
Consulting Editor: Rosemary Ellen Guiley

CHELSEA HOUSE
PUBLISHERS
An imprint of Infobase Publishing

LAKE AND SEA MONSTERS

Copyright ©2008 by Infobase Publishing

Chelsea House
An imprint of Infobase Publishing
132 West 31st Street
New York NY 10001

Library of Congress Cataloging-in-Publication Data
Godfrey, Linda S.
  Lake and sea monsters / Linda S. Godfrey ; consulting editor, Rosemary Ellen Guiley. — 1st ed.
    p. cm. — (Mysteries, legends, and unexplained phenomena)
  Includes bibliographical references and index.
  ISBN-13: 978-0-7910-9393-1 (alk. paper)
  ISBN-10: 0-7910-9393-X (alk. paper)
  1. Sea monsters—Juvenile literature. 2. Animals, Mythical—Juvenile literature. I. Guiley, Rosemary. II. Title.
  QL89.2.S4G63 2008
  001.944—dc22
                          2008006258

Text design by James Scotto-Lavino
Cover design by Ben Peterson

Printed in the United States of America

Bang EJB 10 9 8 7 6 5 4 3 2 1

This book is printed on acid-free paper.

Contents

Foreword

Did you ever have an experience that turned your whole world upside down? Maybe you saw a ghost or a UFO. Perhaps you had an unusual, vivid dream that seemed real. Maybe you suddenly knew that a certain event was going to happen in the future. Or, perhaps you saw a creature or a being that did not fit the description of anything known in the natural world. At first you might have thought your imagination was playing tricks on you. Then, perhaps, you wondered about what you experienced and went looking for an explanation.

Every day and night people have experiences they can't explain. For many people these events are life changing. Their comfort zone of what they can accept as "real" is put to the test. It takes only one such experience for people to question the reality of the mysterious worlds that might exist beyond the one we live in. Perhaps you haven't encountered the unknown, but you have an intense curiosity about it. Either way, by picking up this book, you've started an adventure to explore and learn more, and you've come to the right place! The book you hold has been written by a leading expert in the paranormal—someone who understands unusual experiences and who knows the answers to your questions.

As a seeker of knowledge, you have plenty of company. Mythology, folklore, and records of the past show that human beings have had paranormal experiences throughout history. Even prehistoric cave paintings and gravesites indicate that early humans had concepts of the supernatural and of an afterlife. Humans have always sought to understand paranormal experiences and to put them into a frame of reference that makes sense to us in our daily lives. Some of the greatest minds in history have grappled with questions about the paranormal. For example, Greek philosopher Plato pondered the nature of dreams and how we "travel" during them. Isaac Newton was interested in the esoteric study of alchemy, which has magical elements, and St. Thomas Aquinas explored the nature of angels and spirits. Philosopher William James joined organizations dedicated to psychical research; and even the inventor of the light bulb, Thomas Alva Edison, wanted to build a device that could talk to the dead. More recently, physicists such as David Bohm, Stephen Hawking, William Tiller, and Michio Kaku have developed ideas that may help explain how and why paranormal phenomena happen, and neuroscience researchers like Michael Persinger have explored the nature of consciousness.

Exactly what is a paranormal experience or phenomenon? "Para" is derived from a Latin term for "beyond." So "paranormal" means "beyond normal," or things that do not fit what we experience through our five senses alone and which do not follow the laws we observe in nature and in science. Paranormal experiences and phenomena run the gamut from the awesome and marvelous, such as angels and miracles, to the downright terrifying, such as vampires and werewolves.

Paranormal experiences have been consistent throughout the ages, but explanations of them have changed as societies, cultures, and technologies have changed. For example, our ancestors were much closer to the invisible realms. In times when life was simpler, they saw, felt, and experienced other realities on a daily basis. When night fell, the darkness was thick and quiet, and it was easier to see unusual things, such as ghosts. They had no electricity to keep the night lit up. They had no media for constant communication and entertainment. Travel was difficult. They had more time to notice subtle things that were just beyond their ordinary senses. Few doubted their experiences. They accepted the invisible realms as an extension of ordinary life.

Today, we have many distractions. We are constantly busy, from the time we wake up until we go to bed. The world is full of light and noise 24 hours a day, seven days a week. We have television, the Internet, computer games, and cell phones to keep us busy, busy, busy.

We are ruled by technology and science. Yet, we still have paranormal experiences very similar to those of our ancestors. Because these occurrences do not fit neatly into science and technology, many people think they are illusions, and there are plenty of skeptics always ready to debunk the paranormal and reinforce that idea.

In roughly the past 100 years, though, some scientists have studied the paranormal and attempted to find scientific evidence for it. Psychic phenomena have proven difficult to observe and measure according to scientific standards. However, lack of scientific proof does not mean paranormal experiences do not happen. Courageous scientists are still looking for bridges between science and the supernatural.

My personal experiences are behind my lifelong study of the paranormal. Like many children I had invisible playmates when I was very young, and I saw strange lights in the yard and woods that I instinctively knew were the nature spirits who lived there. Children seem to be very open to paranormal phenomena, but their ability to have these experiences often fades away as they become more involved in the outside world, or, perhaps, as adults tell them not to believe in what they experience, that it's only in their imagination. Even when I was very young, I was puzzled that other people would tell me with great authority that I did not experience what I knew I did.

A major reason for my interest in the paranormal is precognitive dreaming experienced by members of my family. Precognition means "fore knowing," or knowing the future. My mother had a lot of psychic experiences, including dreams of future events. As a teen it seemed amazing to me that dreams could show us the future. I was determined to learn more about this and to have such dreams myself. I found books that explained extrasensory perception, the knowing of information beyond the five senses. I learned about dreams and experimented with them. I taught myself to visit distant places in my dreams and to notice details about them that I could later verify in the physical world. I learned how to send people telepathic messages in dreams and how to receive messages in dreams. Every night became an exciting adventure.

Those interests led me to other areas of the paranormal. Pretty soon I was engrossed in studying all kinds of topics. I learned different techniques for divination, including the Tarot. I learned how to meditate. I took courses to develop my own psychic skills, and I gave psychic readings to others. Everyone has at least some natural psychic ability and can improve it with attention and practice.

Next I turned my attention to the skies, to ufology, and what might be "out there" in space. I studied the lore of angels and fairies. I delved into the dark shadowy realm of demons and monsters. I learned the principles of real magic and spell casting. I undertook investigations of haunted places. I learned how to see auras and do energy healing. I even participated in some formal scientific laboratory experiments for telepathy.

My studies led me to have many kinds of experiences that have enriched my understanding of the paranormal. I cannot say that I can prove anything in scientific terms. It may be some time yet before science and the paranormal stop flirting with each other and really get together. Meanwhile, we can still learn a great deal from our personal experiences. At the very least, our paranormal experiences contribute to our inner wisdom. I encourage others to do the same as I do. Look first for natural explanations of strange phenomena. If natural explanations cannot be found or seem unlikely, consider paranormal explanations. Many paranormal experiences fall into a vague area, where although natural causes might exist, we simply don't know what could explain them. In that case I tell people to trust their intuition that they had a paranormal experience. Sometimes the explanation makes itself known later on.

I have concluded from my studies and experiences that invisible dimensions are layered upon our world, and that many paranormal experiences occur when there are openings between worlds. The doorways often open at unexpected times. You take a trip, visit a haunted place, or have a strange dream—and suddenly reality shifts. You get a glimpse behind the curtain that separates the ordinary from the extraordinary.

The books in this series will introduce you to these exciting and mysterious subjects. You'll learn many things that will astonish you. You'll be given lots of tips for how to explore the paranormal on your own. Paranormal investigation is a popular field, and you don't have to be a scientist or a full-time researcher to explore it. There are many things you can do in your free time. The knowledge you gain from these books will help prepare you for any unusual and unexpected experiences.

As you go deeper into your study of the paranormal, you may come up with new ideas for explanations. That's one of the appealing aspects of paranormal investigation—there is always room for bold ideas. So, keep an open and curious mind, and think big. Mysterious worlds are waiting for you!

—Rosemary Ellen Guiley

Introduction

The bodies of human beings are made of 61.8 percent water, and the planet Earth sloshes at its seams with nearly three-quarters of its surface covered by H_2O. Small wonder, then, that so many creatures of lore and legend spring from lakes, rivers, and seas. Sporting fins, scales, and sometimes horns or fur, a riot of unidentifiable aquatics have poked their dripping heads above the waves throughout recorded history to shock grizzled sailors and hardy fisherfolk alike. But survivors of water monster encounters are usually left as puzzled as they are terrified. Where do these beasts come from, and why are they so elusive? Any schoolchild can describe what a sea monster looks like, yet no museum boasts a skeleton—or even an irrefutable photograph—of a sea serpent or the Loch Ness Monster.

Of course, not all stories of unknown water creatures involve oversized animals. Legends of mermaids and mermen—creatures with human tops and fishy bottoms—swim rampant through the folktales of every country and are still occasionally reported in modern times. Circa 1936, a Norwegian hunter at Cape Horn sighted a green-haired mermaid.[1] Many Native American traditions tell of rivers inhabited by tiny humanoids or "little people" that live alongside mystical water lynxes known as *Mishipeshu*.[2]

Some sightings and even many ancient legends could possibly be explained by either known marine animals or species that are as yet undiscovered. Humanity has not yet documented all of creation; species previously unknown to science are discovered every year. In 2006, 30 previously unknown species of fish were discovered on the island of Borneo alone.[3] Several new species of deep-diving beaked whales have been discovered in the past two decades. The primary scientific evidence for one of them, called Andrew's Beaked Whale, is a series of carcasses that have washed up onto beaches in or near Australia and rare, stranded, live specimens.[4]

Beaked whales even share a few characteristics with the standard sea monster since some of them possess teeth inside a defined, narrow muzzle and lack the telltale bulk of larger whale species. And since beaked whales are rarely seen near the surface, preferring to gulp squid and other prey found near the ocean bed, few people are familiar enough with them to know a beaked whale if they see one. But beaked whales cannot possibly explain the full variety of strange creatures that have been seen, so what other mysterious beasts might still be out there?

Oceanographers admit they've barely begun to explore the vast depths of the seas, and with present knowledge it is impossible to say exactly what might lurk in the deepest regions, the **abyssopelagic zone**, 13,000–20,000 feet below the surface, and **hadal zone**, 20,000–36,200 feet deep, zones of the oceans. Are there strange, giant creatures that live so far off humanity's beaten path that they seem like monsters when people encounter them? If so, it has probably always been that way.

In his book, *Monsters*, author David D. Gilmore discusses the places unidentified beasts are most often said to inhabit: "In every cultural tradition, monsters are said to live in borderline places, inhabiting an 'outside' dimension that is apart from, but parallel to and intersecting the human community. They often live in lairs deep underground, in an unseen dimension as it were, or in watery places like marshes, fens, or swamps."[5]

Few places on earth seem more like an unseen dimension than the lightless ocean bed or the lowest reaches of a deep, murky lake.

And water monsters, like all **cryptids**, or hidden animals, also beg the added question of whether they exist as flesh-and-blood creatures or belong to the shadowy realm of myth and imagination. Unintentional, false monster sightings can happen easily. Almost everyone has had the experience of coming upon a gnarled rock or tree stump and—for one stunned moment—believing it is something else entirely. That mistaken identification can be enhanced when the object is seen in or on a body of water. The waves, ripples, and reflections of sunlight that occur naturally in water can play tricks on the sharpest of eyes. Add in normal surface covers like floating rafts of algae, pond lilies, and other aquatic plants to fuzz things up even more, and the chances of mistaking a log for a monster grow.

Yet, thousands of people over the years have sworn they saw water creatures they could not identify: creatures too large or too weird to believe. Witnesses have observed these creatures as they swim, dive, jump, raise their heads, open toothy jaws, ram boats, paddle, devour prey, or even stare a chosen few humans straight in the eye. Their beastly actions prove they are not tree trunks or mere tricks of light and shadow. Still, it's difficult to imagine how creatures so large could evade scientific scrutiny, especially with modern tools of exploration.

Investigators are often tempted to look to the past to explain the unexplainable. Many sea and lake monsters seem to have very close cousins known from the fossil record. Despite their official extinct status, prehistoric reptiles, fish, amphibians, and aquatic mammals have all been suggested as explanations for everything from the Loch Ness Monster to mythic beasts. Perhaps, the argument goes, a few individuals managed to survive as **relicts** in isolated, favorable spots, and surface now and then to tease people with their presence.

That may seem unlikely, but it has actually occurred. The most famous example of a relict is the resurrection of the coelacanth, a large, snappy species of fish that was presumed to have died out 65 million years ago. Fossils of coelacanths, relatives of the modern lungfish, are abundant in layers from the Devonian period where the first amphibians are found. Coelacanths were believed to have survived only until the end of the Cretaceous Period, when flying pterosaurs and a whole slew of dinosaurs perished. But in 1938 a London museum curator shocked the world when she discovered a live, 127-pound coelacanth in the catch brought up by a sea trawler at Cape Horn, Africa. Other specimens have since been taken in Indonesia, Madagascar, and other points around Africa.

Some protest that the coelacanth's story is a rare example of a true relict, and that it looks too much like a fish to explain giant monster sightings. But there are other examples. The megamouth shark, first discovered in 1976 off Hawaii, can measure up to 18 feet long and feeds by using its huge mouth as a filter to sift tiny sea creatures out of the water. Again, however, its size is the only characteristic that people might find monster-like. Most prehistoric creatures cited as explanations for sea monsters simply don't fill the bill in terms of physical appearance and behavior. Also, climatic conditions were very different in prehistoric times, making it hard to imagine how an animal could survive over so many eons of habitat change. And yet, the coelacanth did.

Others prefer a supernatural rationale for behemoths of the deep, believing that sea and lake monsters are not living creatures at all. The idea that they are water spirits rather than water animals is an old one and is widespread in the traditions of all peoples. Those who choose this explanation today reason that the creatures seem to appear and disappear suddenly, they are very difficult to film or photograph, and they provoke an almost universal, eerie feeling of dread in those who see them. Many cultures have interpreted their appearances as omens of disaster.

There are many conflicting beliefs about these unidentified lake and sea creatures. What *may* safely be said about them is that stories and reports of their appearances are universal, and that there are more examples, theories, and tales regarding their existence than can possibly be covered in one book. Water monsters run the gamut from colossal squids to tiny merpeople (part fish and part human), from scientifically accepted species to exotic beasts that are pure fantasy. And for all the mystery and terror they incite, people do love them . . . from a safe distance.

The 1954 film *Creature from the Black Lagoon* about a gilled, manlike aquatic being is one of the most famous movies of all time. The amphibious Japanese gargantuan, Godzilla, splashed onto the big screen that same year, and has since become an icon of monsterdom. *The Abyss* (1989) was a science fiction thriller that pitted sophisticated human technology in a showdown with an alien, aquatic species. (And yes, there are people who believe sea monsters are related to UFOs.)

The media have offered sillier takes on sea monsters, too; a generation of Americans grew up watching the cartoon antics of *Cecil the Seasick Sea Serpent* and the live-action *Sigmund and the Sea Monsters* by Sid and Marty Krofft, to mention just two classics. On top of countless film and TV water monsters, sea and lake beasties appear in myriad comics, games, and books. Despite the fact that most people will never actually see such a monster, the modern world is awash in mythic sea creatures in every genre of mass media.

To thoroughly explore humanity's fascination with Godzilla, Nessie, and all the other wet wonders of the world, this book will examine ancient legend and myth along with contemporary eyewitness stories and the latest scientific discoveries. Although most encounters with sea and lake monsters will probably never be completely explained, light may still be shed on them in the future as the scientific community learns more about the secrets of the sea. And whether the monsters are myth or reality, they may serve a purpose as gigantic as their bodies if they continue to inspire the worldwide quest for unknown water creatures.

Swimming through Time:
Birth of the Sea Monster

When frost and fire meet, the consequences may be dire. In the ancient lands of Scandinavia, Loki the fire god married Angrboda, the giant goddess of frost and ice. Loki was a shape-shifter, and often used his talents to trick the other gods. Over time his pranks became more menacing and cruel. No wonder then, that the three children Angrboda bore him grew to be dangerous, giant monsters: Fenrir, an oversized wolf with super-strength; **Jormungand** (or Jormungandr), a huge, scaly sea serpent; and Hel, the half-flesh, half-rotted queen of the dead.

The gods were so afraid of the trio's potential for evil that Odin, eldest of all the gods and known for his mastery of wisdom and magic, arranged to have them kidnapped and brought to his fortress, Asgard. Jormungand, which means "wolf serpent," so worried Odin that he immediately grabbed the creature and heaved it into the ocean. With whales and other creatures of the sea for nourishment and nothing to restrain him, Jormungand began to grow. His undulating body became so long that he could encircle the entire globe and still bite his own tail. Fearful sailors called him the Midgard serpent; Midgard was the Norse word for the "middle" world, the land of men between the abode of the gods and the regions of the dead. Now all of the Midgard ocean served as Jormungand's playground.

Jormungand could be as tricky as his father. He was able to take the form of a monstrous cat to fool the thunder god, Thor. Another time he was almost pulled into a fishing boat by Thor, but Thor's companion, a giant named Hymir, cut the line at the last minute to release him.

Jormungand still waits in the ocean depths, according to legend written in the ancient Scandinavian verses called the *Edda*, for the final battle of the gods, Ragnarok. (Some Norse traditions believe Ragnarok happened in the distant past.) At that time, the sea will spit him back onto the land and he will fight Thor. Thor will hurl his hammer at Jormungand's huge, green head and kill him, but before death overtakes him, Jormungand will vomit poison on Thor. Thor will stagger exactly nine paces and then die, too. With the old gods destroyed, a new heaven and earth will come forth.

The sagas of the Norse gods date back at least to the time of the Vikings, between about 750 and 1050 CE. But earlier tales of sea beasts can be discovered in other parts of the world.

LABBU AND LEVIATHAN

The people of Mesopotamia occupy an area of the Middle East often called the cradle of civilization. Chief among the legendary creatures of their homeland was **Labbu**, a sea monster whose snakelike body stretched for 300 miles. Labbu would have been frightening enough had he stayed in the water, but he also developed the terrifying habit of crawling onto land to snack on the local populace. It was said that even the gods feared Labbu, whose stories date back to around 3000 BCE, according to an ancient Sumerian inscription in The Sumerian Epic of Creation and Paradise:

> *In heaven the gods ask in haste,*
> *Who will go and kill Labbu?*
> *He let his clouds rise up,*
> *And slew Labbu.* [6]

Figure 1.1 *An artist's rendering of Jormungand, the ancient sea serpent off-spring of Scandinavian gods Loki and Angrboda.* (Nathan Godfrey)

West of Iraq lies Syria, called Canaan in the Bible, and home to the seagoing Phoenicians. One of its great cities was Ugarit, which lay on the shores of the Mediterranean Sea. Ugarit was a bustling population center and sophisticated metropolis between 1700–1200 BCE, but it was not without its mythic terrors. Ugaritic texts and art portray a hellish variety of monsters and divinities, including the sea god **Yam** who was often described as a serpent, although he sometimes took different forms. One ancient bronze statue of Yam shows him as a slim man encircled by a snake from shoulder to ankle.[7] Yam represented the forces of nature to the Ugaritic people, earning his reputation as a "destructive chaos-monster"[8] with every natural disaster that came upon them. Many sources relate Labbu and Yam to a similar sea monster, **Leviathan**, described in the Hebrew Old Testament. Since all three mythic creatures sprang from the same small corner of the world, it isn't surprising that their legends overlap. Leviathan is sometimes thought of as a massive crocodile, but his description in Job 41 makes him sound more like a traditional dragon:

> *Can you pull in the leviathan with a fishhook or tie down his tongue with a rope? . . .Can you fill his hide with harpoons or his head with fishing spears? . . . His back has rows of shields tightly sealed together; each is so close to the next that no air can pass between . . . His snorting throws out flashes of light; his eyes are like the rays of dawn. Firebrands stream from his mouth; sparks of fire shoot out. Smoke pours from his nostrils as from a boiling pot over a fire of reeds. His breath sets coals ablaze, and flames dart from his mouth . . . When he rises up, the mighty are terrified; they retreat before his thrashing . . . Behind him he leaves a glistening wake; one would think the deep had white hair.*

The Bible describes Leviathan more plainly as a serpent in Isaiah 27:1:

> *In that day, the Lord will punish with his sword, his fierce, great and powerful sword, Leviathan the gliding serpent; Leviathan the coiling serpent; he will slay the monster of the sea.*

Leviathan made a splash outside the Bible as well, especially in the mythology of Canaan. And the book of Enoch, a Hebrew text that dates from the second century BCE or earlier and that is considered sacred Scripture by the Ethiopian Church, mentions Leviathan as a *female* monster that lived "in the abyss over the fountains of waters."[9]

BEASTS OF GREECE AND THE INCREDIBLE OF INDIA

The ancient Greeks were not only expert sailors but lived surrounded by water, and their monster myths reveal their bottomless fascination with the ocean. Legends of strange sea creatures, written by Greek poet Homer, date back to 700 BCE. While the Greek king of the sea, Poseidon, was usually shown as a man, his son, **Triton**, was half-man and half-fish, later called a merman. Triton was feared mainly due to a conch shell he possessed that made a terrifying screech and lashed the sea into towering waves whenever Triton blew on it.

The Greeks believed in kindler, gentler water spirits as well, such as the lovely **naiads**, water nymphs who appeared as attractive young women. Even the naiads, however, were not above luring an unwary man to their home in the depths.

Considerably nastier was the six-headed **Scylla**, a sea nymph-turned-monster who lived in a narrow sea channel. Scylla fed upon large marine mammals and any sailor unlucky enough to drift within her reach. Just the sight of her might have frightened anyone to death; her razor-like teeth grew in rows of three, and she thrashed about on six dog-like sets of limbs. Her six heads sat upon long, snakelike necks that wove and bobbed around one another, while a fishlike tail waved from her hindquarters. Because of the tentacle-like necks, some have wondered if Scylla's image was inspired by glimpses of a giant squid. Whatever Scylla's origin, she was a fearsome addition to any Greek sea traveler's nightmare closet.

Apep: From Ancient Egypt to TV Star

Legends of the deities of ancient Egypt are as old or older than any on the planet and are lavishly packed with a hierarchy of gods and demi-gods. One deity, however, was considered so evil that Egyptian priests conducted an annual ritual to repel and banish it. **Apep**, known to the Greeks as **Apophis**, ruled the oceans as a giant serpent, although he could also appear as a mighty crocodile. Also known as Evil Lizard and Encircler of the Earth, Apep's chief sin was his constant attempt to stop the sun god, Ra, from completing his journey through the sky every day. Apep would wait until Ra's fiery barge had passed the horizon at sundown and then attack from the watery depths of the ocean. Apep was blamed whenever a solar eclipse occurred and also took the heat for violent storms and other natural disasters.

Priests considered containment of Apep so crucial that they wrote a complete manual on the subject, "The Books of Overthrowing Apep." Part of the ritual involved chopping, burning, and spitting upon a wax effigy of Apep, as verses were chanted to leave no question as to his defeat. A sample of the anti-Apep rally from ancient sources reads: "Taste thou death, O Apep, get thee back, retreat, O enemy of Ra, fall down, be repulsed, get back and retreat! I have driven thee back, and I have cut thee in pieces."[10]

Many Egyptian illustrations of Apep show him hacked into many sections or posed in other stages of defeat. The ancient priests would have been astonished to know that some 4,000–5,000 years after Apep was first mentioned in their manuscripts, he would achieve great fame on the other side of the world.

The TV show *Stargate SG-1* (1997–2007), about a United States military team that used an ancient portal to visit other places and times, featured an alien named Apophis who was a lord of the tyrannical, powerful Goa'uld race. Apophis, like other Goa'uld in the show, was based on the Egyptian character bearing his name.[11] As in Egyptian myth, Apophis and

Figure 1.2 *Apep, an ancient Egyptian serpent-god that ruled the seas, is about to be sacrificed.* (Linda Godfrey)

(continues)

(continued)

Ra were enemies. In the myths, Apophis wasn't able to kill Ra, but in *Stargate SG-1*, a U.S. team of experts managed to do what Apep never could, defeating Ra and leaving Apophis free to rampage throughout the universe. The ancient priests of Egypt would have been horrified.

India, home to one of the most ancient civilizations on earth, also identifies serpent-like creatures with the sea in its earliest literature. **Ananta Shesha** (or Sesha), which means "endless serpent," was a massive snake with 100 heads. Considered king of the **nagas**, godlike creatures that were part snake and part human, Ananta Shesha was strong enough to rip a mountain from its base. And he was said to have done just that in order to create an instrument for making ocean waves. Tales of Ananta's epic deeds come from the *Mahabarata*, the Hindu scripture that by tradition was first spoken in 3137 BCE,[12] but was recorded around 200 BCE. It is typical of ancient myths to have a long oral tradition before being recorded on papyrus or carved in stone.

WHICH CAME FIRST, THE MONSTER OR THE MYTH?

After looking at these ancient examples, it is evident the concept of the serpentine sea monster is both universal and timeless. The question modern monster-seekers must ask is whether aquatic chaos demons and mega-snakes are simply ancient myths or descriptions of real creatures glimpsed in the long ago past.

British researcher Paul Harrison says in *Sea Serpents and Lake Monsters of the British Isles*, "Undoubtedly, sea-faring folk did witness giant creatures in the seas and oceans of the world and many were hitherto unknown species. For example, those who encountered the whale for the first time could be forgiven for misinterpreting it as a nemesis of evil, surfacing from the deep to wreak carnage and devastation upon civilization as we know it."[13]

Or did some of the ancient seafarers glimpse species that, unlike the whale, are still unknown to us? Legends often contain a kernel of truth. It's possible that early Greek, Phoenician, Egyptian, and Indian sailors saw the same creatures that baffle monster witnesses today. If the serpent-like creatures spotted around the globe are actually leftovers from prehistoric times, they would have appeared just as strange and mysterious to humans of ancient times as they do to modern people. And if it's easy to understand how a whale could inspire tales of mythic animals, it's even simpler to imagine that a marine dinosaur might have led onlookers to assume they were seeing some furious water god.

Of course, the snake-beasts of the sea were far more than mere potential predators to the people who recorded their stories so carefully. The image of the great serpent in the ocean occurs so frequently across cultures that it may be what Swiss psychologist Carl Jung would have called an **archetype**, or subconscious mental image common to all of humanity. Jung believed that all humans carry within their psyches certain symbols, and that we see these symbols reflected back at us when we look out into the world. It is almost as if we interpret the natural world by our pre-programmed, archetypal software. According to this theory, something has conditioned humans to associate large serpents with bodies of water, and therefore the same creatures seem to pop up wherever humanity wanders.

Researchers may never know all of the religious, historical, and psychological reasons that Leviathan, Labbu, Yam, and Ananta Shesha dominated early oceanic myth or where the first sea serpent image actually came from. But these creatures were very real to the ancients who believed that ocean waves were churned by chaos demons. Perhaps they knew something that modern civilization doesn't. That thought is enough to keep present-day explorers on the lookout for Leviathan's return.

Water Animal Planet: Global Legends

Sturdy brick buildings line downtown Manistee, a once-great lumber town on the eastern shore of Lake Michigan. East of Manistee and south of the Manistee River State Game Area lies little Claybank Lake. Just off a dense national forest, the area is a paradise of woods and water for all wildlife, known or unknown.

A 1987 newspaper article in Traverse City, Michigan's *Record Eagle* recounted an old lumberjack's tale of two fishermen who had tried their luck in Claybank Lake one day. As the sun was about to set, they began packing their lines and lures and were ready to row to shore when they spotted an animal swimming toward them. One of the men owned a coonhound, and the pair figured the dog had somehow gotten loose on shore and plunged into the lake to find his master. But as the supposed coonhound paddled closer, the men realized they were mistaken. What they had taken for a coonhound had a dog's head, but the body looked strangely man-like. The men panicked when the creature began to climb into the boat.

Wielding oars, they clubbed the scary and baffling animal to prevent it from coming aboard. Eventually it gave up and slunk back into the lake and the men were able to row back to shore. Michigan reporter Sheila Wissner later contacted one of the men, but he was still too spooked to talk more about the animal.[14]

Figure 2.1 *Artist's interpretation of the encounter between two fishermen and a dog man in Claybank Lake in Michigan.* (B.M. Nunnelly)

Dog men are not traditionally thought of as lake monsters, but native North Americans have a long tradition of furry water creatures. The ***unktehi***,[15] thought to look like oversized oxen by members of some Plains tribes, are water spirits that may cause people to drown, canoes to tip, or catastrophic floods to threaten villages. The *unktehi* are especially feared because of their favorite food: the spirit or soul of a human being. They may only be defeated by chopping off their tails.

A story in the December 2005 issue of *National Geographic* magazine tells the Cherokee version of this monster, the *unktehila*. It is described as more like a snake than a cow, resembling some of the skeletons of prehistoric marine animals that the Cherokee had discovered around parts of the Badlands for centuries. According to the quoted storyteller, Kevin Locke, the skeletons were proof to his people that these water monsters of their ancient traditions actually once lived there.[16]

Still another source holds that the *unktehila* (or *uktena*) looks like a huge rattlesnake with horns.[17] These river-dwellers breathed poison on humans when disturbed, and the mere sight of one could cause death.

North America is hardly the only place to continue the ancient tradition of water monsters. The only thing more amazing than the wide geographic spread of aquatic unknowns is the sheer variety of forms that they take.

PACIFIC PADDLERS: HONG KONG TO JAPAN

Not all sea monsters are ancient. The **kai kwai** or "sea devil" that slithers around the waters of the Pacific island of Hong Kong was spotted as recently as March 1969,[18] according to author John Keel. A group of university students reported seeing a "big, black creature" on a Hong Kong beach one night that month. The monster made "crying" noises as it popped up from the sea only about 20 feet away from them. The students estimated its length at about 30 feet and added that it had a "big head" with round, green eyes.

Japan, according to traditional belief, is infested with small water monsters called **kappa** that can also go airborne, traveling on flying cucumbers. A sort of vampire, the *kappa* lurks underwater awaiting swimmers and travelers, then sucks their blood after it drags them under. Its appearance is grotesque, with "long hair, the body of a tortoise, scaly limbs and an ape face," according to Jan Knappert's *Pacific Mythology*.[19]

The ape face has a legendary explanation since, according to another source, the *kappa* were once monkeys who served as messengers for the god of the rivers.[20] But probably their weirdest feature of all is the bowl-shaped indentation on the top of the *kappa*'s skull. The dent is used by the *kappa* to carry water. It's an unfortunate feature for the *kappa*, however, since spilling the water from the indentation will cause the creature to lose its magical powers. This problem turns doubly fatal when combined with the *kappa*'s tendency to be very honorable and polite, which in Japan requires frequent bowing. As soon as it bows, of course, the *kappa*'s skull water sloshes out and the creature is at anyone's mercy.

Japan also contains more familiar marine beasts. Dragons, usually thought of as winged lizards by the Western world, are also considered water monsters in Japan and can live in any body of water. Like the *kappa*, Japanese water dragons are **chimeras,** or creatures made of parts from many different types of animals. Covered with fishlike scales, they can rake prey with claws like those of a large cat, and they have heads like those of a horse or camel. Horns of various shapes adorn their brows. They do have wings like dragons of other cultures. But Japanese water dragons also possess the unusual ability to increase or decrease in size. They appear in a variety of colors that are associated with positive virtues like love or courage, although white dragons may signify famine.[21] There is also a **Dragon King** that is considered ruler of all lakes, with the power to drain or refill lakes at will.

Polynesians, people living on a number of islands in the Pacific that include Hawaii, Samoa, and the Marquesas, have traditionally worshipped a god of the sea named **Tangaroa**. Tangaroa was considered the creator of human beings. But Polynesian seas were filled with other water deities and monsters such as **Rongo Mai**, a large whale and the king of all other whales.

Hawaiians have the *mo'oo*, a shiny black lizard up to 30 feet long that inhabits fish ponds. Although their presence in a pond will turn any fish inedible, they are usually considered guardians or protector spirits, and are spoken of in the earliest creation stories. However, they are also shape-shifters, and can disguise themselves as beautiful, alluring women in order to trick unwitting men into the water for their dinner.

Australia possesses a full roster of water creatures. The Aborigines have long believed in a snakelike creature they called the ***devil-devil***. They told E.S. Hall, a European settler who encountered an unknown creature in Lake Bathurst in 1822, that the *devil-devil* was a dangerous monster that preyed on children. Hall and a companion had been washing themselves in the lake and were just getting dressed when the animal came gliding "with the rapidity of a whaleboat" toward them.[22] What they were able to observe was a long neck with a tiny head adorned with "black flaps." After having a look at the men, it plunged back into the water and departed.

This *devil-devil* is just one description of a more general Australian term for aquatic monsters: the **bunyip**. An early printed mention of a bunyip in the *Sydney Gazette* in 1812 says the creature was "seal-like."[23] (E.S. Hall had a second sighting of a bunyip that looked like a seal or dog.) But other descriptions have ranged from a sheepdog-like creature with flippers to a cattle-sized, man-eating creature with sharp claws. One 1848 aboriginal drawing of a bunyip does exist, and according to author Ronan Coghlan, who wrote *A Dictionary of Cryptozoology*, it strongly resembled the prehistoric **diprotodon**. The diprotodon was a **marsupial** the size of a hippo that is believed to have died out around 40,000 years ago, but still inhabited Australia when the first humans arrived. It did have claws on its feet but was not a water animal.

Bunyip reports continued into the twentieth century, including a 1947 sighting of a river creature with remarkable whistling ability and a bunyip with two heads spotted in New South Wales in the 1930s.[24] Other names for the bunyip are *moolgewanke*, *kajanprati*, and *dongus*.[25]

AFRICAN AQUATICS

The continent of Africa is known for its amazing wildlife: tigers, elephants, giraffes, and all the other animals that have become staples of our zoos and circuses. But there are creatures, according to those who have lived there, that have yet to be captured or displayed.

One of the most famous is *Mokele m'bembe*, or "river-stopping monster." A German captain reported it in 1913 as a smooth, elephant-sized creature with "brownish gray skin," a very long neck, and one long tooth.[26] The indigenous people of Cameroon believed that the creature would attack any canoes that came near it, and would kill but not eat the occupants. It has also been reported in the Congo.

An explorer and reptile expert named James Powell made a trip to Gabon in 1976 to investigate the possibility of unknown reptiles. He became friends with a shaman of the Fang people, who told him of a creature called a *n'yamala* that looked very much like a small *apatosaurus*, an extinct, long-necked dinosaur. While it lived in rivers, it was known to emerge from time to time to feed on certain jungle plants.

Powell made several other trips, including one with biologist and author Roy P. Mackal in 1980 to the Northern Congo. They did not see the *mokele m'bembe* or find any direct evidence of it, but they did conduct interviews of local eyewitnesses. Powell and Mackal showed them pictures of a variety of animals, both currently living and extinct, and the witnesses consistently chose representations of long-necked dinosaurs as most closely resembling their water monster. They further informed the team that the creature ranged up to 30 feet in length with a rounded body and long tail.

The search for *mokele m'bembe* has continued to the present day, with many expeditions to Cameroon and around Lake Tele in the Congo. Scientist and cultural anthropologist William Gibbons has made several of them, and has written that because of a Japanese team's 1988 sighting of a large, hump-backed creature in Lake Tele, bobbing along as if munching on water plants, he believes the creatures are real and still hopes to see one.[27]

Gibbons also tells a convincing and astonishing story that he learned from the pygmies who live in the area of Lake Tele and from a missionary named Eugene P. Thomas. Around 1960 the members of the Bangombe tribe managed to spear and kill a *mokele m'bembe* that had long disrupted their fishing harvest. It was about the size of a large elephant and possessed strong claws on all four feet as well as a "comb" atop its head. Although it took some doing due to the animal's size, they eventually were able to butcher the creature and serve it as part of a victory party. However, the pygmies told Gibbons that every person who partook of the beast's flesh died. Gibbons notes that members of these tribes had very short life spans to begin with, and that this incident may have been what started many superstitions about the animal.[28]

Mishipeshu, the Horned Water Panther

Great cats are usually not thought of as especially good swimmers, much less water dwellers. But one of the major players in the creature lore of North America's Ojibwe and Cree people is Mishipeshu, the great water lynx or water panther. Its name has been spelled in myriad ways due to its wide territory, and descriptions can vary, but these tribes believed it to be the special guardian of the ancient copper mines of Michigan's Upper Peninsula. Its home was Michipicoten Island, and taking any of the pure chunks of copper ore from that island was considered strictly taboo. One oft-repeated story is of four Ojibwe who tried to steal copper from Mishipeshu, only to be followed home by the screaming water panther. The trip was fatal for all four thieves.[29]

The curse of Mishipeshu continued as Europeans discovered the fortune in copper nuggets on the Upper Peninsula in the mid-1800s. Ships carrying copper would capsize in sudden storms, such as the one that sank the *Algoma* in 1885 with 45 people aboard. The storms, the Ojibwe believed, were stirred purposely by Mishipeshu. Ten ships were sunk in the area of Isle Royale alone.

Mishipeshu is not alone in his quest to guard the sacred copper. **Mishi Ginabig**, a serpent-like creature that bore antler-like horns and measured the same length as the tallest pine trees, was reportedly spotted in the Great Lakes area in the early 1800s. Both Mishipeshu and Mishi Ginabig are enemies of the great Thunderbird, a spirit-being in the shape of a giant bird, which battles them to restore balance between powers of the water and of the air.

By the time Gibbons began making his own trips to Africa, the native peoples around Lake Tele had become too frightened of the *mokele m'bembe*'s supposed magical powers to reveal to any outsiders exactly where the creature could be found.

And yet, the lure of a possible living dinosaur has continued to attract individual explorers and the media. Although no concrete evidence of its existence has been found, it inspired the 1985 movie *Baby: Secret of the Lost Legend* about living dinosaurs discovered in the Congo. And in May 2006, a National Geographic Channel show called *Dangerous Encounters* filmed an unsuccessful investigation of Lake Tele.

Skeptics believe that those claiming to see *mokele m'bembe* have actually witnessed a crocodile, hippo, or rhinoceros partially camouflaged by the effects of moving water. Believers insist the reports are too widespread to ignore, and that the cave-lined rivers and dense forests of Cameroon and the Congo would provide a perfect habitat for a relict population of undersized sauropods. The pygmies who compete with it for fish have no doubt as to its existence. Perhaps their past experience with eating the beast's flesh will prompt them to bring the next dead *mokele m'bembe* to one of the many eager scientists for the final proof that dinosaurs still walk among us.

Merfolk and Other Scaly Humanoids

$\mathcal{J}$t's hard to say which is scarier to the human psyche: monsters so radically different from *Homo sapiens* that their alien appearance alone makes them terrifying, or monsters that—but for a few scales or fangs—could *be* human.

It's easy to be repulsed by creatures that are clearly not people. But add a lovely face to a fish tail and the monster becomes more complex. Should it be feared or admired? Is it dangerous or friendly? If something that looks almost human may live submerged in water, might a full-fledged human also survive beneath the waves?

Actor Tom Hanks played out that fantasy in the 1984 movie *Splash*. Darryl Hannah starred as a mermaid who saved Hanks from drowning as a boy, and later took him back to her mesmerizingly beautiful world under the sea. And this conclusion seemed a natural one since the mermaid was both human-like and attractive.

MIDDLE EASTERN MERPERSONS

Perhaps that perception of being related to these creatures helps explain humanity's long preoccupation with merpeople: mythic, fish-tailed humans who live in some type of water. Archaeologists have found effigies of the fish-god, **Oannes**, in present-day Iraq that were sculpted by Babylonians more than 7,000 years ago.[30] The story of Oannes is known due to a history of Babylon written in Greek by a Babylonian temple priest named Berossus around 200 BCE. He described how the fish-god came from the Red Sea to teach men everything they needed to know for civilization: writing, mathematics, and agriculture. Oannes did not resemble the modern physical idea of mermaids or mermen, however. He possessed the complete body of a fish, with the additions of a human head above the fish's head and human feet sticking out beneath the tail of the fish's body.[31]

Another early Middle Eastern god was **Dagon** (or Dagan). In the Bible, it was Dagon's temple that Samson brought down after Delilah helped the Philistines capture him. Conforming more closely to modern waterfolk depictions than Oannes, Dagon was shown in ancient art as a classic merman with the upper body of a man and the lower part of a fish.[32]

FISH-TAILED EGYPTIANS AND GREEKS

The ancient Egyptians believed that male and female merpeople originated in the Nile River. Besides fishy tails, these scaled ones were also endowed with muscular human legs and feet with webs between the toes.[33]

The original Greek merman, Triton, roiled the waves with his magical conch shell, as discussed in the first chapter of this book. But there were later merpeople named after him. The Tritons earned their daily minnows by pulling the chariots of Poseidon and the goddess Aphrodite. Some looked like Triton, although a few of them boasted two tails. Others appeared downright monstrous and acted accordingly. One ancient description by second-century Greek traveler Pausanius (quoted in the online resource *Theoi Project: Guide to Greek Mythology*) paints a lurid picture of these creatures:

> "I saw another Triton among the curiosities at Rome, less in size than the one at Tanagra. The Tritones have the following appearance. On their heads they grow hair like

that of marsh frogs not only in colour, but also in the impossibility of separating one hair from another. The rest of their body is rough with fine scales just as is the shark. Under their ears they have gills and a man's nose; but the mouth is broader and the teeth are those of a beast. Their eyes seem to me blue, and they have hands, fingers and nails like the shells of the murex. Under the breast and belly is a tail like a dolphin's instead of feet.

—Pausanias, Guide to Greece 9.20.4"[34]

MODERN MERFOLK AND DEFORMED HUMANS

The notion of aquatic humanoids persisted and mutated through the centuries. Medieval seafaring Europeans sometimes claimed to spot the bizarre monkfish. This weird monster featured a bald, human-like head, scales that hung down in the shape of a monk's robe, and elongated flippers for arms. The sea monk was said to dunk boats and sailors alike into the drink, either by raising a storm or by direct attack, and was much feared. And the monkfish was not the only sea creature with a religious angle. Sailors also sometimes claimed to see the equally strange bishop-fish, which was topped off with a head shaped like a Catholic bishop's mitre (a tall, pointed hat).[35]

At some point, merfolk lost their reputation as monsters and became much more sympathetic characters. Danish author Hans Christian Anderson wrote his story of "The Little Mermaid," who sacrifices her lovely, immortal life for the love of a human prince, in 1836 (today it is known mainly for the animated Disney movie based on the tale). And the Reader's Digest book *Strange Stories, Amazing Facts* includes two earlier legends of appealing merfolk.[36]

The first tale dates to 558 AD, when residents of Northern Ireland heard a woman singing beneath the waves of Belfast Lough. They sent a crew out on the lake to catch her with a net, and learned that she once had been a human child who was plunged into the waters with her family during a catastrophic flood. She was baptized and named

Murgen, or "born in the sea." The townsfolk set up a water tank for her home, and she was said to have done many miracles and was locally worshipped as a saint.

The second legend recounted in that book took place in the Netherlands, a nation infused and surrounded by the North Sea. The sea, with all its tributaries and canals, provided a natural backdrop for water creature legends in this small country. But consider the plight of the merpeople: Once out of their native element of water, they have no way to move about and may end up stranded. That's just what happened in 1403, the story goes, when villagers discovered a beached mermaid covered in "sea-mosse."[37] The mute maid was taken in by kindly women who cleaned her up and took care of her for 15 years. She was finally buried there in holy ground.

Figure 3.1 *Illustration of a merman.* (Nathan Godfrey)

One of the weirdest mermaid reports ever filed was an item from a Pennsylvania newspaper, the *Columbia Spy*, which wrote on March 7, 1863, that a traveler named Hernando Grijalva saw a creature he described as half-monkey, half-fish off the coast of southern California in 1823. According to the article posted by Loren Coleman on the *Cryptomundo* Web site, the creature easily dove and leapt around the boat, and was able to float nearby in a "sitting" position. It was said to have "a dog's head and eyes, arms like a man, breast and body like a woman, with a long tail like a fish and divided at the end like a swallow's tail . . ."[38]

The "sea-ape" was the same color as a porpoise, the article added, and may have had scales on its tail. Grijalva and others observed the animal for more than an hour, he said, and compared its size to that of an otter. They were so impressed with its strange appearance that Grijalva even wondered whether they had actually seen a vision of "the Blessed Virgin,"[39] despite the lack of the creature's resemblance to any known depictions of the revered Christian figure.

If witnesses are to be believed, merfolk still frolic in modern times.

According to Ulrich Magin in a 1992 issue of *Strange Magazine*,[40] a half-woman, half-fish creature was spotted off an island in the South Atlantic in the early 1920s, and a green-haired mermaid was discovered by a Norwegian hunter near Africa's Cape Horn in the mid-1930s. Magin also notes a fishlike female with human legs he said was captured near Yemen in 1973.

The main point of Magin's article, though, is that many creatures touted as mermaids and mermen were really only human beings with birth deformities such as legs fused together or unusual skin conditions. As an example, he cites the October 1950 birth of an Austrian child whom newspapers described as having "head, arms and breasts . . . of a woman, but it had the tail of a fish." The media also called the child a "siren." **Sirens** were originally island bird-maidens of Greek mythology that, over time, evolved into beautiful sea nymphs known for luring seafarers off course, and the word also refers to a class of animals including manatees, dugongs, and sea cows (see sidebar).

"Births of this nature are regularly reported in the papers," said Magin, "and I assume they are due to some genetic deficiency. We can easily understand how, in earlier centuries, they were explained as the result of rape by a water spirit so the unfortunate woman could in some way rationalize the tragic event."[41]

Magin gives other examples, such as a so-called siren born in 1973 in Peru with legs joined by a membrane. The child did not survive and was "discovered" two years later preserved in formaldehyde at the police station in the city of Arequipa.

Manatee or Mermaid?

Attempts to find a natural explanation for the sightings of mermaids and mermen over the ages usually center around a group of animals of the order Sirenia, named for the ancient Greek water nymphs. But anyone looking at a blubbery manatee or its cousins, the dugong and sea cow, might have a tough time imagining how these massive, gray sea beasts could be mistaken for anything even remotely human. With their tiny eyes, split upper lip, and stubby bristles, manatees average about seven feet in length and weigh between 450–1,000 pounds. Dugongs can measure nine feet long, and sea cows, extinct Sirenians that once occupied the waters off Bering Island in the far reaches of the north, could reach 30 feet in length and weighed up to four tons!

It's true that Sirenians hold their young in their flippers to nurse them, much like humans, and that the manatee is a sociable animal. But unlike mermaids, they cannot actually live underwater; they must come up for air every 15 minutes or so.

Manatees live in three main locations: along the Amazon and Orinoco Rivers in South America, between the eastern coastal waters of the United

LEAPIN' LIZARD PEOPLE

There are other types of near-human **aquatic creatures** besides alleged mermaids. In at least two U.S. states, Wisconsin and South Carolina, witnesses have reported a manlike being covered with scales, closer in appearance to a lizard than a fish.

The South Carolina lizard-like biped appeared in a swamp area near Bishopville in 1988, as reported by 17-year-old witness Christopher Davis. The seven-foot creature with dark green scales and four-inch claws hopped onto the teen's car as Davis attempted to flee, and Davis was only able to dislodge it with great difficulty and extreme auto maneuvers.

States and the northern shores of Brazil, and along the western coast of Africa. When some of America's first settlers arrived in Jamestown, Virginia, they were surprised to see manatees in what they later named Manatee Bay. One record from 1739 stated "A Sea-Cow was killed upon Old Woman's Valley beach, as it was lying asleep, by Warrall and Greentree."[42] The animal was probably already dead or dying, as manatees live in water and cannot move on land. This fact also refutes a Mexican superstition that male manatees may steal out of the coastal waters at night and kidnap human females.[43]

It's hard to see how creatures from the Americas and Australia could account for old tales of mermaids seen off European shores or found on beaches. (It's remotely possible, but unlikely due to habitat requirements, that a few of the sea cows that once inhabited the area near Bering Island may have strayed southward.) However, it is possible that sailors near Africa or parts of the New World where these creatures are found might have glimpsed a dugong or manatee coming up for air a long way off and somehow had the impression it was partly human. Perhaps even the ancient Babylonians managed to spy a Sirenian animal somewhere and took it for a fish-god named Oannes.

Wisconsin's lizard man crawled out of the Mississippi River in La-Crosse on the state's western border in 1993 or '94. It surprised a man and his son out hunting for a lost dog one evening along the riverbank. The pair was able to back away as the creature glared at them with slanted yellow eyes, and they estimated its height as taller than the average man. It was covered with "mud-colored" scales.[44] (The dog was eventually found unharmed.)

Both these examples appear to be amphibious rather than strictly water creatures, and they are not the last of this type to be reported at large on the planet. In March 2005 an amphibious man was seen paddling in the Caspian Sea not far from Iran, according to the Russian newspaper *Pravda* (first reported in the Iranian newspaper *Zindagi*). The creature was a pale, whitish color[45] with a protruding belly and had what looked like dark green hair on its head. It was said to have arms with webbed hands.[46] Locals claimed to have seen it for several years swimming near fishing trawlers, from approximately the same time offshore oil production was increased in the area. It was also seen chasing schools of fish. Despite the numerous sightings, no photos or other proof have been offered to date of "Casper," the ghostly-colored merman of the Caspian.

4

Saltwater Serpents

The powerful currents of the Gulf Stream carry life-giving warmth through the oceanic waters south of Florida. And its breezy trade winds have made the area a popular route for sailing vessels since man first figured out how to top a boat with billowing fabric. But the well-used route has claimed its share of casualties. The ancient coral reefs that surround the Florida Keys lie dotted with wrecks of ships large and small that succumbed over the ages to the ocean's perils: storms, pirates, and perhaps one danger a bit less known than the rest.

An unusual sight startled three scientists, all members of the British Zoological Society, one early December day in 1905, as they sailed in the yacht *Valhalla* somewhere south of Key West. The *Valhalla*, named after the mythic Norse hall of the gods, was a 17-ton cruise vessel owned by an aristocratic astronomer, Lord Lindsey, Earl of Crawford. He and his friends E.G.B. Meade-Waldo and M.J. Nicoll all witnessed a six-foot-long fin in a dull green "seaweed" color knife through the water's surface about 100 yards away. Lindsey described it as "somewhat crinkled at the edge," according to an account by James B. Sweeney in his book, *Sea Monsters*.[47]

Lindsey probably almost dropped his binoculars when he saw what came next. He wrote to the respected Zoological Society that, "A great head and neck rose out of the water in front of the frill. The neck appeared about the thickness of a man's body. It was from seven to eight feet out of the water. The head and neck were all of about the same thickness."

Lindsey's companion M.J. Nicoll said the creature's head was like that of a turtle, that it had eyes, and that the head and neck swayed from side to side. Unfortunately, the yacht was traveling at high speeds and soon outdistanced the strange creature, ending the scientists' scrutiny. But a few hours later, two crewmen on the *Valhalla* also glimpsed a huge beast just below the surface of the water. They said they did not know what it was, but it had no blowhole and was not a whale.

The *Valhalla* sighting was widely reported, particularly since the witnesses were considered impeccable due to their scientific standing. But saltwater serpents had been in the news for many years by that time, especially along North America's eastern coastal waters. One of the most famous was the Gloucester serpent, which was sighted a bit farther north in the chillier waters off Massachusetts, in 1817.

The huge and mysterious marine beast was seen so many times, in fact, that a local scientific committee was formed to look into the matter. The group of three men devoted themselves to taking detailed statements from witnesses such as two women and a number of fishermen who all saw a large, unknown creature swim right into the harbor just north of Gloucester at Cape Ann in August of that year. (A similar creature had been sighted in Cape Ann as early as 1639.) Numerous sightings followed in the days and weeks after, including one simultaneous sighting by 20 people.

The investigative group interviewed a Gloucester man named Amos Story who swore that he saw a serpent-like animal in the middle of the day in Gloucester's harbor, and was able to watch it for over an hour as it darted about in the water. The turtle-like head poked about one foot above the water, said Story.[48] "On this day, I did not see more than ten or twelve feet of his body," he added.[49]

Passengers and crew on many ships passing in or out of the harbor continued to see the monster until the end of August, when sightings curiously stopped. The creature returned in October, however, for a few final glimpses. By that time several hundred people had claimed sightings. Not all the reports agreed on the monster's size or appearance, but the general conclusion was that it had a smooth, snakelike body and a horse-sized head shaped like that of a turtle. Most people described the color as very dark brown, and many observed a row of humps following along behind the head. It was said to move its body like a caterpillar, hunching and straightening vertically.

Estimates of its speed varied, since some people observed it swimming rapidly and others saw it at rest. The committee was never able to come to a decision on exactly what the creature was—and indeed the few strange conclusions they did reach brought them only embarrassing, public scorn. For instance, they decided a three-foot blacksnake discovered near the harbor beach must be a "baby sea serpent," and solemnly named the new species *Scoliophis atlanticus*. To their dismay, a reptile specialist who correctly identified the specimen almost immediately proved them wrong.

Further difficulties were caused by the fact that, possibly due to differences in weather, light, and distance, many of the witness reports varied in their recollection of the creature's appearance. This also caused people to ridicule the committee's final report, as skeptics argued that a real creature should have produced more consistent reports. Most researchers today agree, however, that the committee did perform a valuable service in questioning so many witnesses and recording their accounts.

CHECKING OUT CHESSIE

New England's Chesapeake Bay is the site of yet another well-known Atlantic sea creature, nicknamed "**Chessie**." This particular creature is an exciting example of monster lore, partly because Chessie incidents need not be dredged up from ancient documents. The greatest bulk of sightings occurred in the 1980s, and Chessie has even starred in a home video, the subject of which was grudgingly pronounced live by a Smithsonian-sponsored group.

Chesapeake Bay, a huge channel of water that Chessie calls home, slices into Virginia from the Atlantic Ocean near Virginia Beach, then cuts a wide swath north into Maryland. Known for its fisheries, the waters of the great bay could provide plentiful nourishment for a large marine animal. Chessie may be one of the few cryptids, or unknown animal species, that can boast its own page on a state's official Department of Natural Resources Web site, with history, photos, and possible explanations.[50]

According to Maryland's Web site, the sightings go back to at least 1936, when the crew of a military helicopter buzzing the Bush River spotted an unrecognizable, "reptilian" creature slithering through the water below. Other sightings occurred sporadically, but in 1978, a man named Donald Kyker and some of his neighbors saw not one but four serpents! Kyker, formerly with the Central Intelligence Agency, was considered a very credible witness.[51] And in 1980, a woman named Trudy Guthrie saw what might have been a manatee, but which received enough publicity to spark a wave of Chessie sightings.

Then, an amazing break occurred on May 31, 1982, when a serpentine creature showed itself to Maryland residents Robert and Karen Frew. The Frews were able to shoot just under two minutes of videotape of the enigmatic animal as it swam about 100 feet from shore. Members of a Chessie research group called the Enigma Project arranged for the videotape to be examined by a panel of scientists affiliated with the Smithsonian Institute in August 1982. While no definite conclusions were reached regarding Chessie's true characteristics, the group at least conceded that the film showed an "animate" or living object.

Further attempts to identify the animal shown in the film were made by the Johns Hopkins Applied Physics lab in Laurel, Maryland. Technicians made computer enhancements of the creature and revealed an "impressive, unmistakable, serpentine shape."[52] Unfortunately, money for the project ran out before further progress could be made, but the Enigma Project has continued its research.

A Maryland journalist named Bill Burton has also taken up the call to document Chessie's existence and has accumulated 78 reports, according to Maryland's DNR Web site, the most recent occurring in 1995.[53] And according to the site's Chessie fact sheet, most of those witnesses report that Chessie is 20–30 feet long with an elongated neck and a football-shaped head. Chessie is about the thickness of a telephone pole, and ranges from dull green to brown. A few have reported flippers and horns, and Chessie appears unconcerned about humans, with no aggressive behavior observed. Chessie is usually seen on the eastern side of Chesapeake Bay, at dawn or dusk in spring and summer.[54] And at least one enterprising company, Chessie Tours, L.L.C., offers Chessie cruises around the bay. There is reason to hope that one of these tours might produce the next video of Chessie; in 1980, 25 witnesses from four charter boats saw her.

SEA BEASTS AND SUBMARINES

While the U.S. Atlantic coast seems to be a true hotspot for serpent-like, oceangoing animals, modern observations of these creatures are just as far-flung around the globe as ancient sea serpent myths. Some of the strangest—and least known—sightings were made during World War I (1914–1918) by crewmembers of German U-boats, or early submarines. In fact, one U-boat (or undersea boat) may actually have impaled a giant, prehistoric-looking sea monster on its prow!

According to author and oceanographer James B. Sweeney, Germany had dispatched hundreds of U-boats of all different sizes around the world.[55] Because so many were sunk by Allied forces, few of their ship's logs survived, which makes it all the more amazing that so many still recorded seeing large, unidentifiable marine monsters.

A German commander named Schultze made one such report. Schultze wrote that his U-boat and two others were about 30 feet beneath the surface when his vessel suddenly ran into some kind of large object and started to sink, the bow forced downward. With

Figure 4.1 *A German U-boat. During World War I, many U-boats reported sightings of unidentified sea creatures.* (Bettmann/Corbis)

some effort, the crew managed to surface. They immediately rushed to the conning tower to have a look at what they had impacted. To their great shock, they discovered the object that had almost sent them to the ocean's bottom was a giant creature like none they had ever seen.

"It was not a whale," Sweeney quoted from the commander's report. "It had a long neck, body like an elephant and a head resembling a very large turtle. The beast was all of 50 feet in length."[56] The creature was so thoroughly impaled on the submarine's prow that the commander had to send men outside to chop it away piece by piece before they could get underway again.

Another event involving a similar beast proved even more amazing. Another submarine crew surfaced to recharge its batteries, only to discover that a massive marine animal was attempting to clamber onto the U-boat's deck! It was so heavy that it threatened to sink the vessel, forcing the German crew to open fire upon it. The beast finally decided the ocean was a friendlier environment than the submarine deck and slid back into the water. It had damaged the boat so badly, however, that the sub had to remain on the surface where it was easily picked off by a British patrol two days later.

After being captured, the German boat's captain told the British what had happened and described the creature as having "a small head, but with teeth that could be seen glistening in the moonlight."[57]

Sweeney recounts several other sightings, and also mentions a communication proving that the German military suspected the Allies were floating monster-shaped decoys in order to lure them into traps. This shows that large marine beasts must have been appearing with some regularity in the North Atlantic during those war years.

Of course, the Atlantic is not the only ocean on the planet. The Pacific, too, has had its share of seafaring monsters and, like the east coast of the United States, claims its own sea serpent hot spots.

MONTEREY BAY'S OLD MAN OF THE SEA AND BOBO

One notable center of activity is Monterey Bay, off central California. Historian Randall A. Reinstedt spent a lifetime studying not only the numerous shipwrecks off this coastline, but reports of unidentified sea creatures as well. In his book, *Shipwrecks and Sea Monsters of California's Central Coast*, Reinstedt notes that although there are plenty of known sea animals such as whales and many varieties of great fish, two fairly distinct creatures have been reported over and over again that are difficult to explain. One, a serpent-like animal, is known as Monterey's "**Old Man of the Sea**," and the other, described as "elephant-like," is called "**Bobo** the Sea Monster."[58]

Reinstedt makes a case that Monterey Bay is a likely place for large marine creatures to show up, since it contains the Monterey Submarine Canyon, a vast and deep chasm that stretches out into the Pacific Ocean.

It was when the fog rolled in, usually near the mouth of the Salinas River, that Bobo the Sea Monster would poke its massive, bullish head

Identifying the Unidentifiable

Ancient myths paint unknown sea creatures as true monsters, or beings that combine characteristics of different species and that may possess supernatural powers. But the modern view of sea "monsters" is usually that they are unknown, natural animals. But what *kind* of animal are they? Reptile? Amphibian? Mammal? Some researchers have analyzed as many eyewitness accounts as possible and created models that most closely match all these descriptions.

The task itself is monstrous, given the many stories reported over the years by hundreds of people in all types of weather and light conditions, from varied distances and points of view. Creatures that resemble giant whales, squid, or other known ocean dwellers demand separate categories. And those that most closely fit the public's mental image of sea monsters have been described with many combinations of long necks, "humps," flippers, heads ranging from turtle-like to horse-like, lengths from 20 to over 100 feet, and skin both scaled and smooth. Yet most classifiers have managed to boil them down into some basic subtypes.

In 1963 French zoologist Bernard Heuvelmans wrote a classic book, *In the Wake of the Sea Serpents*, that attempted to place sightings from around the world into nine categories: long-necked, merhorse, many-humped, super-otters, many-finned, super-eels, marine saurians, yellow-bellies, and fathers-of-all-the-turtles.[59] While it is now alleged that Heuvelmans skewed data to fit his own ideas in some cases, he is still known as the "father of cryptozoology" for his pioneering work on unknown species.

Inspired partly by Heuvelman's work, scientists Dr. Paul H. LeBlond of the University of British Columbia's Institute of Oceanography and Dr. John Sibert looked at reports of large, unknown creatures inhabiting the waters of British Columbia and found three subtypes that sound much like sea monsters reported around the world. These were repeated in

Figure 4.2 *The three types of unidentified sea creatures described by Dr. Paul LeBlond.* (Linda Godfrey)

a 1980 book by biologist and author Roy P. Mackal, who cautioned that the three categories may not represent separate species and in fact might simply show differences between male and female:

1   A creature with large eyes set laterally on a horse- or camel-shaped head mounted at the end of a long neck. This animal is a fast

(continues)

(continued)

swimmer, has short, dark-brown fur and no mane. It is probably a mammal and may be related to seals.

2   An animal similar to the first type but with small eyes, sometimes described with horns or mane. Both types are not only fast, but also smooth swimmers, submerging vertically as if pulled under.

3   A long, serpentine animal, showing loops of its body above water and swimming fast, with much thrashing. Its head is described as sheeplike with small eyes, and it has a dorsal fin running along part of its back.[60]

Cryptozoologists Loren Coleman and Patrick Huyghe mentioned LeBlond and Sibert's list in their 2003 book on the classification of unknown water animals, *The Field Guide to Lake Monsters, Sea Serpents, and Other Mystery Denizens of the Deep*. Coleman and Huyghe noted that LeBlond later decided that the three categories listed above might be just one creature, after all: "An unknown reptile with mammalian traits."[61]

But Coleman and Huyghe, after undertaking a massive study of the best-supported sightings worldwide, came up with a 14-part identification

from the water and let forth a trumpeting bellow from its inflated trunk. Witnesses who saw him either from shore or from a boat said he had large, red eyes that glowed, small fins, and a snakelike body. But Reinstedt appeared satisfied with the verdict of a local scientist that Bobo was nothing more than a stray elephant seal, a massive animal that can weigh as much as two tons.

The Old Man of the Sea was a little harder to account for. Descriptions over the years stuck to a fairly consistent pattern, said Reinstedt. Most witnesses agreed it had a "long, thin, snakelike body, system for unknown aquatics. It includes sea and lake monsters, as well as many types (mystery salamander, giant beaver, and giant octopus) that do not sound much like the long-necked sea monster. Their *Field Guide* puts the "general serpentine form of unknown aquatic animals"[62] into one classification, the **classic sea serpent**.

The lumpier, flippered types are given their own category, **water horses**, which are divided into two types: the long neck, smooth skinned, and slightly smaller at 30 to 70 feet long; and the merhorse, with whiskers, a mane, and a greater size that can reach 100 feet in length. "We understand that a few of these categories may seem to involve creatures of myth and legend," explain Coleman and Huyghe. "But we have based all our types on a careful examination of long-term evidence of a biological nature."[63]

These categories will probably continue to evolve for as long as these creatures remain a mystery to humankind. In the meantime, they provide a framework, at least, that can be compared and contrasted with new sightings. And if and when the first irrefutable water horse or classic sea serpent evidence finally turns up, any of the monster classifiers lucky enough to still be around will probably not care whether every detail of their categories match the actual creature. They and every sea monster witness through history will finally be vindicated.

and an evil-appearing human-like head." Its length was estimated between about 50 and 150 feet long, and its color said to be dark gray with lighter markings. It also had a "mane" of red hair, said witnesses, and would often rise eight feet or so out of the water to stare at boaters with "mournful" expressions.[59] Although Reinstedt thinks some scientists may be correct in assuming the Old Man is actually an oarfish, which has a red, modified dorsal fin that could look like hair, and which can grow to 50 feet in length, the creature itself is no less astonishing for its possible identification. As Reinstedt says,

Figure 4.3 *The oarfish's serpent-like appearance and long, red dorsal fin led scientists to believe that it was the true Old Man of the Sea.* (Linda Godfrey)

" . . . the possibility cannot be discounted that at one time there could have been fish in Monterey Bay that boasted flaming red manes, were snake-like in appearance, and grew to monstrous proportions!"[65]

Kraken, Giant Squids, and Octopuses

It was a calm day at sea, and we sat bobbing in the waters off West Africa whilst we waited for the wind to fill our sails and send us on our way. The captain, Jean-Magnus Dens, would suffer no idleness on the part of his crew, and we Danes like to keep our vessels seaworthy. Therefore it pleased him to set us to work scraping barnacles and other such filth from the hull.

We strung sturdy planks on heavy rope, then lowered the planks down the outer edge of the hull so the men could stand and scrub away. We thought we were safe from sharks and such other creatures, but we were not counting on what lurked near us on that day of ill portent.

It delivered no warning; a big and terrible head with eyes like saucers rose fast from the deep. It waved its devilish arms at two of the men on the planks and then grabbed them. Two hearty mates, pulled under the sea in the blink of a seagull's eye! I had a good look at the beast from where I stood on the deck, and there was nothing I could do to bring those men back above the foam. The captain—I remember his eyes grew almost as big as the monster's—shouted for harpoons. But before the men could fetch them, another arm came whipping out of the water like a hungry snake and curled itself around the fellow standing next to me. He screamed like a mountain troll and hung onto the rigging while I grabbed me a hatchet and struck the arm for all I was worth until it cleaved in two and the stump slid back into the sea.

*We quickly unwrapped the beast's severed arm from the sailor but he had fainted dead away and some say he was crazy in the head from that time on. We measured the cut-off arm at 25 feet, and that wasn't the whole of it. The harpooners had at last got five spears driven deep into the monster's body but it snapped every line as if it were tailor's thread. No one had to tell us we had met up with a **kraken**, the ocean monster that grows to the length of 10 men and more. We felt much sorrow for the lives of those two good sailors. They died unspeakable deaths.*

NORSE ROOTS OF THE KRAKEN

This dramatization based on an event recorded by a Danish sailing ship in the late 1800s is echoed by other seafarer's stories of encounters with giant squid or octopuses. But scientists of the day had a

Figure 5.1 *Stories of the kraken, or the giant squid or octopus, have circulated since the sixteenth century.* (Troy Therrien)

hard time believing that giant **cephalopods,** a class of creatures that literally means "head-foot" and also includes the cuttlefish and nautilus, truly exist.

Stories of the kraken originated in Norway. A Swedish clergyman named Olaus Magnus wrote of the kraken as early as 1523. The name was derived from the word for a stunted tree, as sights of the creature floating and waving its tentacles reminded early chroniclers of a stump with its roots in the air.[66] At first "kraken" was applied to any large, unknown sea creature, but it later became synonymous with the giant squid or octopus.[67]

A story is told that dates back to 1680 of a kraken that accidentally snagged itself on some craggy rocks near the Norwegian shores and then starved to death. The sickening smell of the giant, decaying carcass wafted on the ocean breeze for miles and lasted many months, driving the local populace from the area until the odor abated.[68]

GONE CRACKERS OVER KRAKEN

Stories of encounters with kraken kept trickling in from amazed seamen, leading French naturalist Pierre Denys de Montfort to believe they were real and natural creatures. He classified the alleged sailor-snatcher as a species of giant octopus when he wrote *Historie Naturalle Générale et Particulière des Mollusques* (The Natural History of Mollusks) but was laughed at by other scientists. Smarting from the ridicule, he set out to prove the creature's existence. He spent much of his life interviewing whalers and other seamen, and eventually came to St. Malo, a port city in northwestern France. He had heard that a painting of a strange sea monster hung in the town chapel. It showed a scene very similar to the Danish ship's encounter: a monstrous cephalopod with two arms curled over the ship's masts, crewmen furiously hacking at the arms with axes to free themselves. And as in the case of the Danish ship, the incident portrayed in the painting also took place off the coast of West Africa. The crew had commissioned the painting when they returned home as thanks to their patron saint for saving them.

Denys de Montfort may have gone a little off the deep end at this point, however. He had an exaggerated copy made of the painting and published it as proof of the giant cephalopod's existence, only to be called a fraud and charlatan. He died a pauper around 1820 and never achieved his goal of proving the creatures were real.

GIANT SQUID REVEALED

Ironically, just a few decades later, in 1857, a Dane named Johan Steenstrup published a paper on the giant squid based on parts of a specimen caught in Jutland, Denmark. He named it *Architeuthis*. Steenstrup's work was not widely accepted right away, but before two more decades had passed, concrete proof of the species finally surfaced. A beached giant squid—60 feet long—turned up in Newfoundland, and was surpassed a few years later in 1880 by another found in New Zealand that measured 65 feet from one end of the body to the tip of the longest tentacle. (However, one biologist has cautioned that the length of giant squids may be exaggerated if the tentacles are stretched out "like rubber bands" at the time of measurement.[69])

Such carcasses are still being found today. A squid "As Big as a Bus," according to one national headline,[70] washed up on a beach off southern Australia in July 2007. The animal weighed 550 pounds and measured 26 feet long. Another newspaper article in the same month noted that a species known as the Humboldt squid, with an average weight of 100 pounds, has become commonplace in Monterey Bay, California. The Humboldt was formerly known to live much farther south near South America and Mexico, where it goes by the name of "Red Devil," *diablo roja* in Spanish.[71]

The largest of another species of super-squid, the Colossal Squid or *Mesonychoteuthis hamiltoni*, was taken off the coast of New Zealand in February 2007. It was 33 feet long and weighed 990 pounds. The

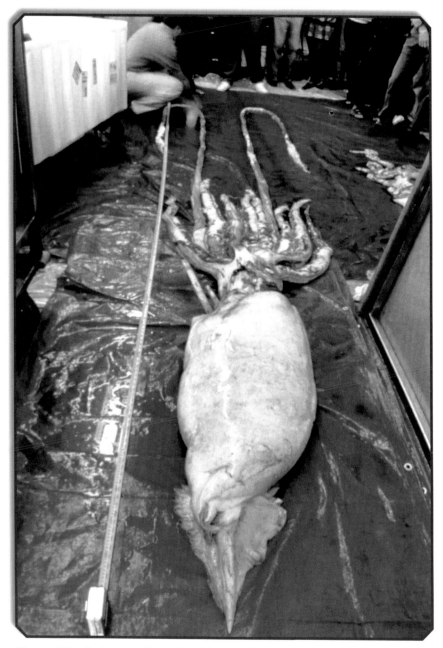

Figure 5.2 *A giant squid weighing 250 pounds and measuring 25 feet in length being prepared for display at the American Museum of Natural History in New York.* (Reuters/Corbis)

squid, when caught, was busy chomping on a Patagonian toothfish caught on the line of fishermen working in the Ross Sea for a sea-food company. As humans cover and explore more of the world's oceans, giant squid and octopus records will undoubtedly continue to shatter.

That has scientists excited, because cephalopods are a strange and fascinating class of marine animals. They are thought to be the most intelligent of invertebrates, or animals without backbones, and can manage feats of weird biology such as changing color and squirting ink to escape from enemies.

Dracula of the Sea: The Vampire Squid from Hell

Colored a dark, blood red, with 10 limbs and huge eyes that are larger in relation to its body than any other known living animal, the **vampire squid** is seldom seen by humans because it lives in one of the deepest regions of the ocean, sometimes 3,000 feet or more below the surface. It wasn't even discovered and classified until 1913, when marine biologists baffled by the creature's strangeness gave it its own order. Its weird characteristics put it somewhere between the squid and the octopus families, and its species name, *Vampyroteuthis infernalis,* means "vampire from hell."

Two of the hellish creature's arms are unlike those of a normal squid because they are proportionately longer—twice the length—and are suckerless. The vampire squid keeps them rolled up in two pouches and shoots them out when needed, perhaps to use as feelers or to grab prey. Its prey, by the way, would not be man, even if humans could somehow manage to swim at that great depth. The vampire squid only averages six to eight inches in length, yet its eyeballs are about the same size as those of a Rottweiler!

GIANT SQUID VERSUS GIANT OCTOPUS

While the giant squid and giant octopus may seem very similar at first glance, they do have some major differences. The giant Pacific octopus, *Enteroctopus dofleini*, is the largest octopus species and, while not reaching the sizes of the largest squids, can weigh up to 600 pounds. A 156-pound specimen taken off British Columbia in 1967 measured 23 feet long.[72]

A close look reveals the anatomical differences between squid and octopuses. Octopuses, or octopods (the scientific community prefers

Unlike octopuses or other squid, the vampire squid has no ink sac. But it does sport rows of sharp, tooth-like needles along the sides of its arms. The little cephalopod is also very speedy for its size, and can turn and maneuver on a dime . . . or perhaps, on a doubloon from some old pirate's treasure. When threatened, it turns itself inside out so that the spiny arms, connected by webbing, form a protective covering around its head and body that is eerily reminiscent of Dracula's cape.

But perhaps the vampire squid's best trick is its ability to turn itself on and off like a light bulb by covering and uncovering bioluminescent, circular organs called **photophores** with flaps of skin. With its photophores hidden, it could swim virtually invisible in the dark regions it inhabits, then open the flaps to appear in the blink of an eye. It is thought to use the photophores as part of its defense against larger animals, opening and closing them and emitting showers of lighted particles to confuse predators.

Luckily for squid enthusiasts, there is no need to hire deep-sea diving equipment for a look at a vampire squid in action. One of the feisty creatures was caught on video and has become a star of the Web site YouTube at http://www.youtube.com/watch?v=q5ZQH2Uzpew.

Figure 5.3 *The Giant Pacific Octopus is the largest octopus species. On average, they are 16 feet long and weigh 50 to 90 pounds.* (Jeffrey L. Rotman/Corbis)

either to the term octopi), have eight arms, each equipped with one or two rows of suckers. Squids also have eight arms, but in addition possess two tentacles that may be lined with hooks or sucker rings. Squids also have two or more fins.

Squid and octopuses still have much in common. Both have mouths inside the base of their arms, the easier to feed themselves. And probably the oddest thing about both creatures is the way they are assembled, with their limbs attached directly to their heads, and their bodies (containing visceral organs) on the other side of their heads. They also have three hearts and beaks shaped much like a parrot's, used for clamping onto prey. It's little wonder these huge and multiarmed creatures have become known as the "real" sea monsters.

6

Lake Lurkers

On a sunny morning in the late 1980s, two teenaged boys approached the muddy backwaters of the swollen Ohio River in Henderson County, Kentucky, armed with a .22 caliber pistol. The boys, Andy and Mike, planned to take turns shooting turtles off logs, and soon found targets aplenty. Mike's father, who had driven them to the isolated spot, remained in his car but was close enough to hear the shots from the handgun.

The shooting stopped, however, when Andy saw something bob up from the river only a few yards away: a green hump, like an auto tire, covered in moss with dark green circles the size of baseballs spaced about a foot apart. Both boys watched in amazement as another hump surfaced close to the first one, and then another, until five humps sat there like a string of tires tied together. The humps were segmented and their surface resembled the skin of a lizard.

The greatest shock, however, came when a head rose from the water in front of the humps. The boys could clearly see its elongated snout and dark, black eyes. As the head swung in their direction the creature appeared startled and sank quickly, humps and all, beneath the surface.

This account was adapted from *Mysterious Kentucky*, with permission of the author, B.M. Nunnelly, who interviewed Andy some years after the incident occurred; Nunnelly found that the memory was still fresh in Andy's mind.[73] Andy added that the creature (later named

Genny, for the Geneva area in which it was sighted) was approximately 30 feet long and as big around as an automobile tire. It did not have scales. Andy also noted that a dark line ran along the creature's length, and that when the beast disappeared from view, it sank swiftly all at once rather than plunging forward in a diving motion. The creature swam with a side-to-side movement (unlike most serpent sightings which are usually described as up-and-down motions) that created a powerful wake. Andy also told Nunnelly that both he and Mike were too stunned to even think of firing at the creature, which appeared large enough to have made the boys its dinner if it had cared to. Andy was able to direct Nunnelly, a skilled artist, to create the drawing that accompanies this story.

To this day, says Nunnelly, Mike is still too unnerved by the incident to talk about it. But Nunnelly has uncovered other eyewitnesses in the Geneva area. In 2001 James Kennedy was spending his Fourth of July holiday camping in the Sloughs Wildlife Management Area only two miles from Mike and Andy's encounter. To his surprise, he was able to watch a large, unknown "snakelike" creature swim as close as three or four feet from shore for several hours. The animal was no behemoth, measuring only about three feet long, but it had a beak shaped like a duck's and swam with its head above the surface of the water. Kennedy told Nunnelly he was close enough to be sure that it was not a snake, and regretted that he had failed to bring his net along to try to capture it. It's tempting to speculate that this was an offspring of the larger creature seen by the two teenagers almost 20 years earlier. Or perhaps there is more than one type of unknown aquatic inhabiting the area around Geneva, Kentucky.

Nunnelly has also witnessed a few strange things in the waters of that state. One incident occurred about 20 miles from the two spots mentioned above, when he was able to view a humped, duckbilled, snakelike creature that he estimated at somewhere between the size of the two previously sighted creatures. This sighting was also made in the Ohio River, near Stanley in Davies County. His wife also saw

Figure 6.1 *Using direction from an eyewitness, B.M. Nunnelly was able to create this sketch of Genny.* (B.M. Nunnelly)

it, and the couple was able to observe it for 30 minutes as it swam and repeatedly dipped from sight in the same, swift sinking motion noticed by Andy and Mike.

In the mid-'90s, as he drove across a bridge over the Ohio, Nunnelly saw the neck and head of an unknown aquatic creature. It rose about five feet from the water, and reminded him of pictures he had seen of that famous Scottish lake monster, **Nessie** of Loch Ness.

Nunnelly recounts other sightings of unidentified lake animals in his book, *Mysterious Kentucky*, making it seem that the Bluegrass State has a corner on spooky, swimming serpents. Not so. Lake monster reports occur all over the United States and world in at least 1,000 locations, according to a tally by researchers Loren Coleman and Patrick Huyghe.[74] In fact, there exists a history of monster lore in another lake named Geneva, in Wisconsin, and its resident creature is also called **Jenny**.

JENNY OF GENEVA LAKE, WISCONSIN

Sightings of Jenny in Geneva Lake near Wisconsin's Illinois border go farther back in time than those of Genny in Kentucky.

Geneva Lake, a popular vacation destination for Illinois tourists since the late 1800s, is Wisconsin's second deepest lake with spots 142 feet deep. With an eight and a half-mile square surface, it is fed by underground springs, considered by some Native Americans to be doorways to the spirit world. And in September 1902 the *Milwaukee Sentinel* reported that a serpent-like creature had appeared in Geneva Lake the previous Wednesday afternoon and was witnessed by a total of six people. Two women and two men first saw it "coiling" near shore, but when the men rowed out for a better look, the creature instantly sank beneath the waves. According to this author in *Strange Wisconsin*,[75] the group estimated the creature to be 65 feet long, about the size of a local steamship. A highly respected minister also reported an encounter with the creature that year.

A few years earlier in July 1892, the *Chicago Tribune* reported that two boys and a man named Ed Fay saw a fearsome reptile while fishing from a boat. The three witnessed a huge head rise from the lake with jaws opened wide to reveal needle-sharp teeth. The massive head towered 10 feet above the water, topping a long body covered with scales that ranged from pale green at the belly to dark brown at the tail. The serpent was judged to be 100 feet long and three feet around. And the group's nightmare continued as the beast chased them to shore, then turned back across the lake, making "bizarre sounds" as it swam. Hordes of people flocked from Chicago to Lake Geneva in hopes of seeing the monster. According to historian Paul B. Jenkins,[76] the Potawatomi who lived in three villages around the shore at the time of the settlers also insisted the lake hid an eel-shaped lake monster.

THE ODDITY OF OGOPOGO

So many serpent-like creatures have been reported in freshwater lakes that to adequately report them all would take many volumes. But a few well-known favorites command regular attention. One of the most widely recognized is **Ogopogo,** the monster of Okanagan Lake in southern British Columbia. A Department of Recreation and Conservation sign on the shore of Okanagan declares that a monster known to Native Americans as **N'ha-a-itk** had inhabited its waters long before the coming of Europeans.

N'ha-a-itk eventually became Ogopogo, which, surprisingly, is not a Native American word. The name was invented by a British Rotary Club member for a song parody in 1926 and adopted by British Columbians the same year for the Okanagan creature.

Written reports of Ogopogo go back to 1850, says a comprehensive article in *Mysteries of Mind, Space & Time: the Unexplained.*[77] But the first glimpse to cause a big stir was claimed by a steamer captain in July 1890. He described a serpentine animal 15 feet in length with a sheep-like head and fins. Others continued to spot the creature over the years, reporting that it had a long neck, a dark green, blue, or black color, and humps similar to those of the Ohio River creature described by Kentucky witnesses.

The Shushwap Indians, who threw animal sacrifices into Okanagan Lake to ensure the creature would spare their canoes, left a rock carving of their idea of the beast. It depicted a horse-headed, long-necked animal with fins or flippers, a slender body, and a slightly fanned tail.

Several films and photographs have been made over the years that purport to show Ogopogo swimming through the lake, but all have been disputed. Still, a film made on an eight-millimeter ciné camera by Art Folden in 1968 of a 60-foot creature was analyzed with modern techniques in 2000. Analysts agreed it showed something solid sticking out of the surface in three places, including what appeared to be a head and a tail.

Figure 6.2 *A model of Ogopogo, a lake monster seen in Okanagan Lake in British Columbia for centuries.* (Fortean PictureLibrary)

A video made in 1980 by Larry Thal presented an object of about the same size as Folden's, and another in 1989 made by Ken Chaplin caught a smooth, green, spotted creature about 15 feet in length. Chaplin's film was featured in *Time* magazine and examined by a wildlife expert who declared the film indeed showed some living creature, but probably a beaver![78] Chaplin, however, insisted that what he saw from 75 feet away was furless and reptilian.

Arlene Gaal, a local journalist and author who has written three books on Ogopogo and claims to own 99.9 percent of the Ogopogo photos in existence, has also stated the Chaplin image is not a beaver. To date there is no shortage of people trying to shoot the film that will prove "Ogie's" existence. The first person to capture unarguable, scientific proof will earn not only fame but also a $2 million (Canadian) reward.

CHAMPING AT THE BIT: MONSTERS OF NEW YORK, SWEDEN, AND OTHER PLACES

Another famous lake monster has long been spotted in Lake Champlain, which borders New York State. P.T. Barnum once offered $50,000 for "**Champ**'s" body, and in July 2006, ABC News obtained a video of Champ shot by two fishermen on a digital camera. The two men saw various parts of the monster—a head, the nose—as thick as a man's thigh emerge from the water. ABC News had the video examined by a forensic image analyst, who could find no evidence that the images had been manipulated. But the analyst couldn't prove any part of it to be an animal, either.

In 1873 Champ was alleged to have caused a steamship accident when a boat ran into the round-headed, snakelike creature and was almost swamped. Champ emerged again in 1883, when spotted by a sheriff, and in 1887, when seen by a farm boy and a small group of people. Almost a century later, two separate incidents in the 1970s prompted sonar and submarine studies of the lake, but no proof of the lake creature resulted.

In central Sweden, Lake Storsjön is the home of a creature known as *Storsjoodjuret,* said to have lived there for more than 350 years. A Swedish society dedicated to investigating the creature has collected hundreds of reports. A typical, multi-humped serpent with a long neck and "horse's mane," *Storsjoodjuret* was spotted by a family of three in 1985, and has also been hunted with submarines and other technology to little avail.[79]

The most famous lake monster in the world is Nessie of Loch Ness in Scotland (see next chapter), but similar creatures have also been discovered in the lakes, or *loughs,* of Ireland. A small lake near the sea in County Galway, Lough Abisdealy, is said to harbor an eellike or snakelike creature. Three people who saw it in 1914 described it as "long and black, with a long neck and a flat head, and three loops of its body buckled in and out of the water as it traveled quickly across the

Hunting the Elusive Lake Monster

So you want to take your passion for **dracontology**, the study of lake and sea monsters, to the field. Monster hunters have been searching for proof of sea and lake monsters—physical remains, detailed photos or film, a snippet of a fin for DNA analysis—for a very long time in every conceivable body of water. While some may debate the wisdom of this practice, given the overall lack of success so far, the hunt for sea monster evidence is unlikely to be abandoned any time soon. The only question then must be: What is the best way to go about looking for unknown aquatics?

The first order of business is to locate a lake or seashore with a history of credible sightings. This may require opening a big can of whup-research. There are many sites on the Internet devoted to compilations of sea and lake monster sightings, and a few books with extensive listings that may be found in libraries or online. But your own, original research can turn up exciting new areas to explore. Check old local newspapers (some libraries retain local "clipping" files of unusual subjects) or seek out longtime area sportsmen and interview them about unusual activities in local lakes. Any known eyewitnesses should also be interviewed if possible.

A study of the geographical area you intend to visit, including what type of vegetation and terrain surrounds the body of water, is a must. It's also extremely important to learn what known fish and other animals are normally found in the vicinity so that you don't mistake an alligator for a Nessie.

Once at your lake or sea of choice, access to a boat, canoe, or other vessel appropriate to the body of water is always helpful. But many valid sightings have been made from the shore, and today's powerful optical tools, such as telephoto lenses, provide excellent views of distant subjects. It's a good idea to bring an arsenal of audio-visual equipment to record both sights and sounds. A packing list might include

- video-camera with long-range optical zoom lens
- high-powered binoculars, preferably with camera built in
- digital and film cameras with long-range lenses
- extra batteries
- plastic bags, latex gloves, and tweezers for gathering physical evidence
- casting material (plaster of Paris or resin) for shoreline footprints
- field notebook and pens or pencils, plus a waterproof case or plastic bag to keep everything dry
- audio cassette recorder and many tapes
- ruler or tape measure
- global positioning device for recording precise locations
- camp comforts such as folding chairs, food, water, and insect repellent

Be prepared for a long, tedious, and possibly uneventful watch. Most sightings are few and far between. A little research on the creature's most common times of appearance could tilt the odds in your favor. And if you are traveling, don't forget to check the weather conditions of the area so that you can bring the proper outdoor gear. Nothing ruins an expedition faster than needless suffering from excess cold, heat, or rain.

The next level of investigation, of course, involves heading into the creature's own turf: underwater exploration. One Canadian creature-seeker, Jacques Boisvert, made around 2,000 scuba dives in Lake Memphremagog, between Canada and Vermont, in search of the lake creature known as **Memphre**.[80] Boisvert wasn't able to catch so much as a glimpse of the "long-necked, dragon-headed creature."[81] However, that doesn't

(continues)

(continued)

mean someone else won't have better luck in another place and time. Scuba diving isn't for everyone, though. It requires expensive equipment and professional instruction, and is not permitted at every location. Snorkeling is cheaper and easier than diving, but also much more limited in scope and in number of suitable places.

There are other techniques for seeing what lurks below. Although beyond the financial reach of most casual investigators, submarines and sonar sweeps have been used to systematically explore the bottoms of many lakes where monsters are reported to hide. But investigators who lack the connections or wallets to arrange tech-heavy events should not despair; most of the subs and sound-wave blitzes have yielded only ambiguous blips, while surface watchers armed only with hand-held cameras have recorded many images worthy of serious study.

In the joyful event that you do witness an unidentifiable creature, be sure to record every possible facet of the encounter, including date, time of day, weather conditions, position of the sun or moon (can help account for glare or unexplained flashes in photos), other people or animals in the vicinity, direction the creature was headed, and every detail of the creature itself: estimated size, color, shape, features, behavior, and motion. Do not be afraid to mention any intuitive feelings you may have, although you should label them as such.

A few caveats: Always make sure that you have legal right or permission to be on the viewing or boat-launching property, and be aware of any dangerous wildlife that may be in the area and take appropriate precautions. Remember, too, that many more people have succumbed to the dangers of water itself—undertows, rip tides, boating and diving accidents—than to the spiky teeth or lashing tails of elusive mystery serpents. Safety first!

Figure 6.3 *View of Lake Champlain, alleged habitat for the lake monster named Champ.* (James P. Blair/Corbis)

lake . . ."[82] Another witness estimated the creature's length at 25 feet, and said its color was dark brown.

Even just from these few examples, it's interesting to notice the close resemblance that lake monsters around the world bear to one another: slender, snakelike bodies, long necks, blunt-nosed heads that remind people of mammals like horses or sheep, and often flippers or fins. Some have bulkier bodies and short limbs, but both body types are also consistent with the main types of creatures reported in saltwater or marine environments (excluding those of the tentacled variety), especially those in Coleman and Huyghe's *Field Guide*: the classic sea serpent (slender-bodied) and the water horse (thick-bodied).[83]

But as usual with unknown creatures, the question of whether lake monsters truly exist comes down to the testimony of eyewitnesses and some inconclusive film and photo records. It could be argued that if pranksters or hoaxers had made all these sightings, it's unlikely the reports would remain so consistent, regardless of time or location. Or did early accounts of sightings influence later descriptions by people who were preconditioned to see giant snakes after reading about them in newspapers? Only Nessie, Champ, and Ogopogo know for sure.

Nessie: Scotland's
Sea Monster Superstar

Forming a worm-shaped, watery slash across the northern face of Scotland, the legendary Loch Ness outsizes all other freshwater lakes in the United Kingdom. Travelers from Inverness to Fort Augustus must skirt the 24-mile-long lake surrounded by steep mountains and vegetation, passing historic landmarks such as the ancient ruins of Urquhart Castle on the northern shore. Many who make this lakeside trip keep their eyes peeled in hope of spotting the famed occupant of the **loch**: a long-necked creature nicknamed "Nessie" said to inhabit these waters since the sixth century. Some witnesses have seen a long neck snaking over the dark, **peat**-filled water; others have spied one or more large humps gliding across the loch's surface. Most sightings have been made from a distance, leaving room for argument over what the creature might be.

One of the most complete descriptions of Nessie was reported during a flurry of sightings in 1933. A London banker and his wife, Mr. and Mrs. George Spicer, had an eye-popping encounter about 4 p.m. as they headed south on Lakeshore Drive in the middle of July. The Spicers had just vacationed in Inverness, and may have seen a May 2 newspaper article in the *Inverness Courier* telling of a recent Loch Ness water monster sighting. The *Courier* had reported that an Inverness businessman and his wife saw something with a body "resembling that of a whale"[84] creating a great, frothy disturbance on the otherwise placid waters. But the creature the Spicers described was no whale.

They said that as they drove along the lake that summer afternoon, they saw a huge, dark-colored creature suddenly plunge out of the roadside ferns with some kind of small, four-legged prey clamped tightly in its jaws. Spicer estimated the great beast's length at between 25 and 30 feet and noted the creature possessed a surprisingly small head atop a long, sinuous neck. Its body, however, was large and clumsy, and it shuffled rapidly across the road on appendages that looked more like flippers than feet. Spicer said the creature was "horrible—an abomination."[85] The astonished couple watched it disappear into the plant growth on the opposite side of the road, then heard a big splash as it dove back into Loch Ness with its dinner.

The Spicers decided to go public about their experience, and their story appeared in newspapers worldwide. Not everyone believed them, of course, and their claims are still controversial today. Tony Harmsworth's Web site devoted to the Loch Ness Monster calls their story "almost certainly fraudulent."[86] But whether the Spicers were telling the truth or not, others have claimed to have glimpsed Nessie for centuries.

LOCH OF AGES: THE HISTORIC NESSIE

The earliest recorded Nessie encounter was told by St. Adamnan, a church historian who documented the life and miracles of sixth-century Saint Columba about 100 years after Columba's life.[87] Columba was an Irish, Christian missionary who had been working in the northern sector of Scotland for two years when he stumbled upon a gruesome scene at Loch Ness in the year 565. (Some scholars say this did not happen at Loch Ness but at the juncture of the ocean and River Ness.)[88] There he found villagers holding a funeral for a man who had been attacked by a big monster as he swam in Loch Ness. The monster also threatened another swimmer as he attempted to retrieve a boat on the opposite shore. This swimmer later described the creature as "something like a huge frog, only it was not a frog."[89] But the swimmer might not have lived to talk about the gape-mouthed behemoth if the Saint hadn't rescued him by commanding the creature to leave. The monster instantly obeyed St. Columba, and the legend of the Loch Ness Monster was born.

Nessie resurfaced from time to time after Columba's triumph, her reputation surviving mainly in folk tales whispered among local residents until modern communications brought the stories to a wider audience in the mid-1800s. In 1863, a gamekeeper for a local estate vowed that he saw a great "fish" in the loch. A man diving near a submerged shipwreck in 1880 claimed to see the creature swim right past him underwater. Another witness of that time called the lake monster a "noted demon."[90] These tales were widely reported.

The Spicer story set off a long cascade of monster sightings. Author Angus Hall estimates in *Monsters and Mythic Beasts* that around 3,000 people claimed to see the creature between 1933 and 1974.[91] A man named Alexander Ross insisted that he saw Nessie no fewer than three times in 1933. Bounties were placed on the creature's head: $40,000 was offered by a circus and $10,000 by the Bronx Zoo in New York City.

The world was thrilled to learn in December of that same year that a big-game hunter had discovered footprints of an air-breathing, unknown animal whose body he judged to measure about 20 feet long. But the hunter, Marmaduke A. Wetherell, was unmasked as a hoaxer when it was learned the four identical prints had been stamped into the mud with the preserved foot of a hippo.

WHEN SEEING IS NOT BELIEVING: THE SURGEON'S PHOTOGRAPH

A world-famous 1934 photograph that purported to show Nessie swimming with her head and neck poking out of the loch is now also largely considered a hoax. Known as the "Surgeon's Photograph" because it was presented to the *London Daily Mail* newspaper by Dr.

R. Kenneth Wilson, it was immediately suspected as a prank because of the date: April 1, or April Fool's Day. Scientific examination of the prints could not prove or disprove the photo, though, leaving believers and skeptics to argue for decades. The photo might have been disputed for all eternity if not for two Nessie researchers, Alastair Boyd and David Martin.

Boyd and Martin, both members of the Loch Ness and Morar Research Project, wrote a book in 1994 called *Nessie: The Surgeon's Photograph Exposed.* Their book revealed that the famous photo was not only faked, but was not even shot by Dr. Wilson!

The *Nova Online* Web site explains that Martin found a 1975 newspaper article in which Ian Wetherell, son of the man accused of the hippopotamus footprint fakery, claimed that the Surgeon's Photograph

Figure 7.1 *The famous 1934 "Surgeon's Photograph" of Nessie. The photo was later shown to be a fake.* (Mary Evans/Mary Evans ILN Pictures)

was merely an act of revenge by his father.[92] The elder Wetherell, it seems, conspired with Ian Wetherell and his stepbrother, Christian Spurling, to photograph a toy submarine in Loch Ness and sell it to the *London Daily Mail* through the well-respected Dr. Wilson.

Boyd and Martin were able to interview Spurling at age 93. Spurling described how he had created a tiny monster head on the toy sub's tower, and his confession was enough to persuade most people that the photo was not what it had been cracked up to be. However, believers have continued to snap blurry photos of objects in Loch Ness ever since, and many have made the point that even if the Surgeon's Photograph is fake, it doesn't necessarily mean that the creature is, too. Ironically, despite his part in the "unmasking" of the photo, Alastair Boyd is one of Nessie's biggest boosters and made his own sighting in 1979.

NEITHER FISH NOR FOWL? GUESSING AT NESSIE

Those who are convinced that something larger than the average fish really does live in Loch Ness have come up with an abundance of theories. One of the most popular ideas is that Nessie is actually a prehistoric, aquatic animal called a plesiosaur, a creature that closely matches the Spicers' description of the beast that crossed the road. The main problem with this idea is that the plesiosaur has been extinct for 65 million years (see sidebar).

Other researchers have suggested Nessie could actually be a long-snouted Baltic sturgeon, an out-of-place porpoise, an elongated seal, a string of otters swimming in a straight line (creating the appearance of a series of humps), a type of whale, shadows, or even a floating log spewed from the depths by a narrow, standing wave of water called a **seiche**. Some think that although the lake has been shown to be too small to support the breeding population that would be required to keep a monster family thriving (estimated at between 30–50 individuals), undiscovered undersea caverns and connections to the North Sea

The Plesiosaur, if You Please

Few prehistoric creatures come as close to matching the Spicer couple's physical description of Nessie as the long-necked plesiosaurs. These bulbous-bodied, flippered marine reptiles popped into the fossil record 220 to 175 million years ago, and they continued to flourish and adapt until about 65 million years ago when, it is assumed, they went extinct. Plesiosaurs came in a variety of species over the millennia, some with very long and slender necks, and others, called pliosaurs, with shorter necks and long heads. They ranged in size from about eight to just under 50 feet long!

It may have been the resemblance of the long-necked species to the famous "Surgeon's Photograph" that led people to suggest that Loch Ness contains a relict plesiosaur. But studies of fossil specimens, some discovered as recently as 2002, have caused zoologists to speculate that it might have been very difficult for a plesiosaur to hold its narrow neck out of the water while swimming. The neck would tend to bob forward due to gravity.

On the Web site, "The Plesiosaur Site," scholar and plesiosaur expert Richard Forrest says, "The long neck, being mainly bone and muscle will be denser than water, and denser than the main body which contains lungs, and a digestive system generating gasses. This would tend to make the head sink, and lead to a great waste of energy in trying to keep it up."[93] The long neck would work admirably well, however, for foraging the sea bottom or surveying the surface from below.

Given its long rule of the prehistoric seas, the plesiosaur was a very successful animal in its time. Might it have been even more successful than scientists think, with a few individuals still cavorting along the bottom of Loch Ness?

Forrest, along with most other experts, thinks not. Plesiosaurs needed to breathe air, and sightings would be much more common in the Loch than they are since the animals would need to surface regularly. He also

Figure 7.2 *Some suggest that the Loch Ness Monster is actually a relict plesiosaur.* (Linda Godfrey)

notes that Loch Ness is too cold for a marine reptile, that the lake is only 10,000 years old and the plesiosaurs went extinct 65 million years ago, and that its body shape does not match sightings that describe undulating humps in the water. True believers answer that the plesiosaur could have adapted over time to changing water temperature, that it could

(continues)

> *(continued)*
>
> have entered the Loch through underground passageways, and that the humps might have been formed by its back and tail.
>
> Loch Ness is not the only place where plesiosaurs are thought to roam. They have been claimed for many other water habitats around the world wherever monsters have been sighted. But until a live or well-preserved dead plesiosaur presents itself for human inspection, most scientific investigators will continue to consider it strictly a predator of the past.

could provide a habitat for a family of large marine creatures. That also would help explain how a 2003 sonar sweep using satellite navigation and conducted of the entire lake by the BBC[94] could fail to turn up any sign of Nessie. She might simply have been lounging in an adjacent cavern or cruising at sea.

Another line of thought states Nessie doesn't need a breeding population because she is not a physical being. Scotland has a tradition of a mythic creature called a **kelpie**, or water horse. Kelpies were said to lurk alongside lake or river trails, appearing as a beautiful horse that stood saddled and ready to ride. But the instant a hapless traveler mounted the alluring creature, it would dash into the water, revert to its true form, and dine on its rider.

Whatever Nessie is, the towns around Loch Ness know a good thing when it swims by. The village of Drumnadrochit advertises the "Original Loch Ness Visitor's Center," which offers boat cruises and a variety of Nessie tourist paraphernalia. The rest of the local economy also benefits from the hordes of monster-seekers who come hoping for a glimpse of the lake's mascot.

Chances that a good photo may be taken of Nessie have increased in modern times with more and more people trying to capture a "money" shot of the monster. On June 9, 2007, organizers of a music event called "Rock Ness" handed out 50,000 cameras to attendees in the hope that one might catch an image of the lake serpent. Just a week before that, a bounty of $1 million British pounds was offered for Nessie's capture. If Nessie ever is discovered to be a real creature, perhaps the find will not be made by scientists but by one of the millions of visitors who have made the Loch a must-see destination.

Monsters that Were
and Still May Be

The great thing about sea and lake monsters is that they are so much more plausible than, say, vampires or werewolves. For one thing, so much of the world's water habitat is still unexplored that it seems entirely possible that unknown sea creatures could exist in those vast depths. For another, we know that the sea produces some mighty strange creatures like the vampire squid and exotic jellyfish. With creatures like those in our oceans, it seems anything is possible.

But most tantalizing of all is the realization that creatures very close in appearance to sea serpents and water monsters glimpsed in modern times once lived very successfully on this planet and are known from fossil records. Many investigators have speculated that some of them still lurk in the deep trenches of the ocean or the rocky beds of glacier-carved lakes, to occasionally surface and be misidentified as sea monsters.

If that is true, it is easy to see how ancient myths might have evolved from encounters with living fossils. It's also evident that these creatures would look monstrous and out-of-place today. And as the story of the coelacanth (a living species thought to exist 65 million years ago) in this book's introduction demonstrated, it is entirely possible for creatures thought extinct to somehow hang on and show up like time travelers from days *way* bygone.

BLASTS FROM THE PAST: MOSASAURS, BARYONYX, ZEUGLODONS, AND ICHTHYOSAURS

In 1780 a dinosaur jaw was discovered in a mine near the Maas River in the Netherlands. Napoleon had it carted to France in 1795 where it became the object of much discussion for years, as scientists argued whether it was from a toothed whale, alligator, or lizard. Its resemblance to lizards was finally officially recognized in 1822 when it was given the genus name ***mosasaurus,*** which means "Maas River lizard."[95]

Mosasaurs could reach 40 feet or more in length. They looked very similar to Coleman and Huyghe's drawing of the classic sea serpent"[96] with a long, alligator-like jaw and strong flippers on a mostly tubular body. One artist's interpretation of the mososaur known as ***tylosaurus*** also shows it with a scalloped dorsal (back) fin, which could provide another explanation of the short humps sometimes seen trailing behind a monstrous head.[97] It lived in a sea that once covered the midsection of North America, and it ate diving birds, fish, and other mosasaurs.

Tylosaurus was supposed to have died out 65 million years ago. But did it? The state of Utah has become known for sightings of monsters in Bear, Sevier, Fish, Utah, and Great Salt Lakes. Living things can be tenacious. And *Natural History* magazine has noted several paleontologists maintain that "snakes and mosasaurs are more closely related to each other than either group is to any other group of lizards."[98] In that case, calling a mosasaur a "sea serpent" does not seem such a stretch.

Baryonyx was another gator-jawed creature whose fossil skeleton was first discovered in 1983 in a clay pit in the United Kingdom. The lizard-like bones were found about three-quarters complete and would have measured 20 feet long. Evidence shows that *Baryonyx* was a fish-eater and probably used its oversized, deadly claws to hook its prey.[99] The odds may be less likely that this killing machine has survived until the present without detection, since it would probably wreak noticeable havoc wherever it popped up. *Baryonyx* would

Figure 8.1 *Artist's rendering of a Baryonyx, a prehistoric sea predator.* (Troy Therrien)

surely be termed a "water monster" if encountered by some unwary fisherman today.

Another ancient species that ranks high on the possible relict popularity scale is not a reptile at all. ***Zeuglodon*** was a primitive, toothed whale that lived around 25 million years ago and could reach lengths of 70 feet. *Zeuglodon* did not look much like modern whales; it was originally named ***Basilosaurus*** because it resembled a lizard in some ways. But its later placement in the whale category has also been disputed because it has many characteristics of the seal family, or **pinnipeds,** as well. Author Dr. Roy P. Mackal has proposed that an unknown creature observed snatching a duck from a watery surface near Vancouver in 1934 matched what we know of *Zeuglodons* perfectly. "Even a casual comparison," says Mackal, ". . . reveals the striking agreement with the description of the observed animal."[100]

The observed animal, according to the duck hunters who saw it, was about 40 feet long and two to three feet wide with a tapering body and a three-foot-long head. The head was described as horse-like, though lacking ears or nostrils, and as dark, grayish brown marked with one horizontal, dark stripe. This is a description that could match many water creature sightings from around the world, making *Zeuglodon* a prime suspect in the relict category.

Zeuglodon was also tapped to explain one of the most famous sea serpent sightings ever—that of the H.M.S *Daedalus* in August 1848, off St. Helena, a British island in the South Atlantic Ocean. That monster was described by one witness as "a blunt-nosed animal with a neck carried about four feet above the water, which was so long as to present the appearance of a serpent . . . Two or three years after this, on reading the description of a *Zeuglodon cetoides* . . . it struck me that the animal seen from the *Daedalus* may have been a descendent of the order to which *Zeuglodon* belonged; and I have ever since watched with interest for reports of the 'great sea-serpent.'"[101]

While there are probably innumerable prehistoric creatures that resembled traditional sea serpents, with many still possibly undiscovered, one other is often inserted into the lineup of suspected sea monsters: the **ichthyosaur**, which means "fish-lizard." The first ichthyosaur skull was found and recognized off Southern England in 1811. Ichthyosaurs varied in size and appearance from three to over 30 feet long, and from early, eel-shaped species to later versions that looked like dolphins with long, sharp beaks full of teeth. Ichthyosaurs, like mosasaurs, were reptiles, and needed to come to the surface to breathe. But they were more ancient than the mosasaurs, making it even less likely that some of them might have survived until present times.

AND GODZILLA, TOO . . .

An exciting addition to the fossil posse came in 2005 when *National Geographic News* announced evidence—a weird and large skull—of a 13-foot marine crocodile found in 1996 in Argentina and named *Dakosaurus andiniensis*. The skull dated from the Jurassic period, and was estimated to be 135 million years old. Researchers dubbed it

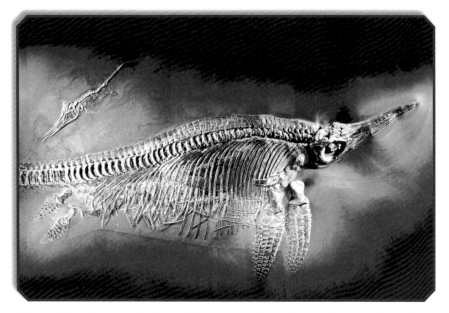

Figure 8.2 *Shale fossil of an Ichthyosaur mother with an infant and five unborn babies.* (Jonathan Blair/Corbis)

"Godzilla" after the colossal sea creature of Japanese movie monster fame because of its huge jaws equipped with rows of serrated teeth. In fact, the online newspaper's headline read, "'Godzilla' Fossils Reveal Real-Life Sea Monster."[102]

GLOBSTERS: REMAINS OF THE DAY

Some extinct species are considered likelier than others to have survived in isolated locations. As noted in the sidebar in Chapter Seven, the plesiosaur is the prehistoric water creature most often pointed to as the relict species responsible for sightings of Nessie and other thick-bodied, long-necked sea and lake creatures. One of the last of the plesiosaurs to show up in the fossil record, *Elasmosaurus*, measured about 60 feet, a length often cited by modern witnesses. It looked much like a seagoing *Apatosaurus*, but with flipper-like feet.

Some have even claimed that freshly dead plesiosaur carcasses have, in fact, been recovered. A giant catch accidentally hauled in by a Japanese trawler in 1977 off the coast of New Zealand caused world excitement because the netted carcass looked much like a plesiosaur. The crew disposed of the rotting animal, but not before one of them took photos, saved tissue samples, and made measurements. It was discovered to be 33 feet in length, and possessed flippers, a long neck, and relatively tiny head.

The Fishapod: A Leaf Off the Old Family Tree?

"Our Cousin the **Fishapod**."[103] That was the headline of an April 2006 article in *Time* magazine announcing a possible ancestral link between prehistoric sea monsters and human beings. Fossil remains of the nine-foot-long creature with characteristics of both land and sea animals were found on Ellesmere Island, Canada, by a team headed by Chicago paleontologist Neil Shubin in July 2005. The creature appeared to have fishlike teeth, gills, and scales, but a head that resembled a crocodile noggin, a rib cage large enough to have held lungs, and instead of flippers, primitive five-fingered hands! "You're looking at your great-great-great-great cousin," said Shubin in the article.

The fishapod lived 375 million years ago, and is thought to have developed in the dawn of the marshy floodplains of rivers during the Devonian period when the first land plants began to take hold and diversify. These shallow, muddy areas provided ideal habitat and new types of food for a creature itching to evolve into a landlubber. Scientists gave the fishapod the official name of *Tiktaalik roseae*, which combines the Inuit language with Latin to mean "large red fish in stream."

Later that year, tests of the tissue samples showed that the remains were most closely related to some type of shark, probably the basking shark. Basking sharks can grow to over 40 feet, ranking them as the second largest true fish. They dine by swimming with their mouths open and filtering small creatures through their gills. According to an article by Glen J. Kuban that first appeared in a 1997 journal, *Reports of the National Center for Science Education*, "When the basking shark decays, the jaws and loosely attached gill arches fall away first, leaving the appearance of a long neck and small head. All or part of the tail . . . and/or the dorsal fin may also slough away before the better supported pectoral and pelvic fins, creating a form that superficially resembles a plesiosaur."[104]

Kuban notes that basking shark carcasses have often been mistaken for sea monsters in the past. So have decayed remains of giant squid, octopus, jellyfish, whales, and other big sea creatures, usually dubbed "**globsters**" because with skin and other outer structures decayed, they look like giant globs lying on the beach. Perhaps someday a similar carcass will turn up in a place known for plesiosaur-like sightings that will finally pass the DNA test. Monster hunters can only hope.

9

Mistake or Fake: Natural Creatures and Hoaxes

". . . the cruel beauty of the salt world, the barnacle's tiny knives, the sharp spine of the urchin, the stinger of the sun jelly, the claw of the crab."
—*E.B. White, "The Sea and the Wind that Blows,"*
Essays of E.B. White

The lakes and oceans are full of an astonishing variety of creatures, each with its own system of offense and defense. Creatures with stingers, claws, or giant mouths full of teeth, especially when man-sized or larger, are sometimes called monsters even if they are identifiable by science. Other times, they and even more innocuous beasts are simply mistaken for monsters by well-meaning people.

The city of Delavan in southern Wisconsin has a small lake near its downtown area that was once the scene of a multi-witness lake monster sighting. The lake adjoins a cemetery. On May 11, 1911, the *Delavan Enterprise* reported that several ladies who had gone to the cemetery to visit a grave said they saw what they called a "mammoth sea serpent."[105] They and the cemetery's gravedigger watched in amazement as the creature repeatedly broke the surface of the water to spout water like a whale. They said its head was shaped like that of a horse, and it left a long wake which made the observers think that the creature must measure dozens of feet in length.

They were right about one thing: the creature's head was horse-like. The creature *was* a horse. It had escaped from its pasture and was trying to swim the lake to find better grazing, but the lake was full of weeds. Unable to swim normally through the underwater tangles, it had to resort to a labored "horse-paddle" and evidently took in water each time it submerged. The water then had to be blown out at each surfacing, which caused the spouting monster effect. The people of Delavan had a good laugh over the incident.

If so mundane an animal as a horse can be mistaken for a sea monster, it seems likely that many more monster reports were also caused by wrong perceptions of familiar and unfamiliar creatures. And there are many known animals that bear closer resemblance to a sea serpent than does a horse.

ELECTRIFYING EELS

In June 2007 a farm family in Hunterton County, New Jersey, discovered a toothy skull the size of a human head, but resembling nothing they had ever seen. Even local wildlife experts couldn't tell them what it was. But eventually, they learned the misplaced skull belonged to a **wolf eel**, a large creature at home in both the Pacific and North Atlantic Oceans. Wolf eels have long, eellike bodies and big heads full of strong teeth designed to crush large shellfish. Adult wolf eels generally live on the bottom of ocean shelf areas, usually staying under a favorite rock or crevice, but it would be easy to mistake a full-grown, seven-foot-long wolf eel for a strange monster, even if just a skeleton were found.

True eels provide some even likelier contenders. In 2004 a Scottish scuba diver named George Telfer was exploring an old shipwreck off Andrew Island when attacked by a 12-foot conger eel that seemed to appear from nowhere. The eel bit his hand and began to drag him away. He was only able to escape by squeezing the 250-pound eel hard with his free hand, but not before the eel slammed him against the wreckage several times, bruising the 42-year-old man's face.[106]

Figure 9.1 *The Wolf Eel could easily be confused with a sea monster.* (Brandon D. Cole/Corbis)

The conger eel also has a dorsal fin, a feature often attributed to sea monsters, along its back. It does not, however, have a long neck, nor does it swim in the type of vertical motion that would produce humps in the water.

OARFISH AND SEA SNAKES: TALL TAILS

Another top contender for sea monster look-alike is the oarfish. Also known as the ribbonfish because of its slim, sinuous body, the oarfish is the longest known bony fish and can reach up to 50 feet in length! Although its normal home is about 3,000 feet below the surface in the Mediterranean and East Atlantic, the oarfish does come to the surface when in distress. The oarfish also boasts a bright red "mane" or crest, actually a modified dorsal fin, along the top edge of its body. This feature has often been included in descriptions of sea monsters.

And on the rare occasions that oarfish have been seen swimming near the surface, they have been observed to move in a snakelike, undulating motion. This bundle of characteristics would fit many a sea monster scenario.

Even more serpentine than oarfish are the aquatic serpents, or sea snakes. Sea snakes breathe air, so they usually live in tropical, shallow waters and need to come to the surface where they may easily be sighted. A variety called Stoke's sea snake can grow to almost seven feet in length, not nearly as long as the oarfish but still large enough to give a startled onlooker pause. They are covered with scales and have the typical, blunt-nosed head expected of any snake. Although sea snakes are venomous, they are seldom aggressive toward man. But since fear of even small snakes seems to be inborn in humans, the sight of a large one in an unexpected place could be expected to provoke thoughts of monsters.

FIERCE FISH: STURGEON AND GAR

Some of the most obvious creatures likely to be mistaken for a sea monster, given their natural habitat, would be true fish. And there are a couple of species both weird and large enough to inspire a bit of monster mania. The large and ponderous sturgeon is certainly one of them. An armor-plated living fossil that has been around since the dinosaurs, the sturgeon is found around the world and includes many species. Its eggs, especially those of the Beluga variety, are highly coveted as caviar. But Beluga sturgeon can grow up to 15 feet in length and weigh 2,000–3,000 pounds. Sturgeon also grow distinctive, bony plates along their back and have pointed, chisel-like snouts designed to nudge food off lake and sea bottoms.

Another fish that looks the part of fearsome, unknown water creature is the alligator gar, second in size only to the sturgeon among freshwater fish in North America. A fierce predator, it possesses something the bottom-feeding sturgeon does not: teeth. Its cone-shaped choppers are set into a long, primitive-looking beak, which can snap up prey in an instant. Their long, sinuous bodies can grow to lengths of around 10 feet and weigh more than 300 pounds.

MORE POSSIBLE CULPRITS "SEAL" THE DEAL

Many other ingenious solutions to the sea monster puzzle have been suggested over the years. A.C. Oudemans, author of the classic 1892 book, *The Great Sea-Serpent*, included a chapter titled, "The various explanations hitherto given."[107] The first explanation he mentions is the opinion of a "gentleman of intelligence" that multi-humped sea monsters are in reality a row of leaping porpoises, following one another in a line. Oudemans notes, however, that no one has ever reported a sea serpent with a separate back fin on each hump, as would be the case if each hump were one dolphin. Oudemans also doubted that dolphins would ever swim in such a tight formation for a sustained period of time.

Figure 9.2 *The Alligator Gar.* (Sea World of California/Corbis)

Other suggestions repeated by Oudemans, besides those already pondered in this and preceding chapters, included very large tuna fish, a row of basking sharks, a row of sperm whales, a stray boa constrictor, a large elephant seal, a gigantic clump of seaweed detached from the sea bed or a coral reef, a mass of birds flying low over the water, a massive turtle, a floating log, and a manatee or sea cow.[108]

One explanation in favor with contemporary sea serpent researchers such as Loren Coleman[109] is that of an unknown, huge, long-necked variety of pinniped, or seal. Oudemans, after taking all other explanations into account and analyzing a huge number of physical and behavioral descriptions as well as geographical data, suggested that the animal that best fit the whole shebang would be a member of the seal family that had adapted to marine life. Oudemans summed up a very long and exhaustive comparison of the characteristics of both sea monsters and seals when he said, "... *at all events the sea serpent is a true Pinniped.* It has four flappers, a hairy skin, and strong whiskers. Its head resembles that of a sea-lion, its long neck resembles that of a sea-lion, its trunk and its foreflappers resemble those of a sea-lion."[110]

ONE BORN EVERY MINUTE: HOAXING FOR FUN AND PROFIT

Not all cases of mistaken identity are simple errors; some reports of sea monsters have been the result of intentional hoaxes. Perpetrators have ranged from simple pranksters to sideshow hucksters.

Decades before the Wisconsin "horse-headed serpent" incident, an even bigger monster stir took place in northwestern New York state in 1855. Researcher and author John Keel tells about the debacle in *The Complete Guide to Mysterious Beings.*[111]

It was on a Friday, the 13th, one July evening that year when a group of fishermen on Silver Lake spotted an 80- to 100-foot, serpent-like creature that they first mistook for a log. The creature was seen by a different group the following night, and continued to make encore appearances. The copper-colored creature had a head the size of a calf's, said witnesses, and a finned back. Before long, the story of the Silver Lake Serpent hit the newspapers and both the lake and the quiet, nearby community of Perry were mobbed by monster-seekers. Hunters armed with harpoons and water bird decoys swarmed over the lake in hopes of catching the monster.

The sightings continued for a year, and then in 1857, a local resort caught fire and was partly burned down. This resort, the Walker House, had profited greatly from the throngs who came to see the monster and in fact hid a secret that was exposed by the fire. The charred remains of a great fake sea monster were found in the hotel ruins, revealing the monster's true source at last. The owner of the Walker House, A.B. Walker, quickly hotfooted it out of town for his own safety, although he returned some years later and was forgiven.

The Perry newspaper reported that the monster was actually the result of a plot of several hotel owners hoping to drum up business. They based their fabrication on an ancient Native American legend of a monster in Silver Lake. The faux water beast was made in a nearby tannery out of waterproof canvas and pumped up by forcing air into an attached hose with a bellows hidden in a lake shanty. As soon as the operator stopped pumping the giant bellows, the creature would lose air and sink back into the lake. Eventually the group became fearful they would be found out and stuffed their creation into Walker's attic. Perhaps they planned to bring it out later if business became slow again. But more than one of them probably wished it would have burned to ashes along with the hotel.

As for the town of Perry, it not only forgave Walker but began holding annual sea serpent festivals that as late as 2007 featured massive balloon liftoffs, as well. The balloons couldn't be more appropriate reminders of Walker's hoax: fabric behemoths sustained by a lot of hot air.

STEP RIGHT UP, FOLKS: MERMAIDS AND SIDESHOW SPECIALS

It's true that no known skeletons or preserved carcasses of present-day sea monsters exist. But facts like that are never enough to deter a showman out to make a buck on the gullible public. In the 1800s, about the same time that tales of sea monsters, both enormous serpents and smaller mer-beings, were becoming rampant around Europe and the Americas, curiously cobbled "proofs" began turning up.

In 1822, a London newspaper ran a letter from a British minister stating he had seen the preserved corpse of a "mermaid" captured off

How a Jenny Haniver Is Made

While it would be almost impossible to fool large crowds today with mummified animal remains glued together to resemble a mermaid—P.T. Barnum's tricks are simply too well known—it is instructive to learn how these nasty-looking critters are manufactured. Richard Ellis, in his book, *Monsters of the Sea*, gives instructions for those with access to fresh sea creatures.[112] While this author would never recommend using sea animals for trickery, seeing how it is done helps ensure that fewer people will be taken in by such things in the future, and hopefully the lives of a few innocent skates and rays will be saved. The summary of the technique, similarly presented by Ellis in the interest of full sideshow disclosure, is as follows:

1 The first step, says Ellis, is to catch a ray, skate, or guitarfish (and presumably kill and clean it.)

2 Next, the animal's fins should be cut to look like wings.

3 Create a neck by tying a string around the appropriate place under the head.

the coast of Japan. It was said to possess a hairy head resembling a baboon's, with the lower body of a scaly fish. It was in the possession of a Captain Eades of Boston.

Upon Eades's arrival in London, a respected museum conservator named William Clift was allowed to examine the dried, leathery remains. Clift had no doubt that the alleged mermaid was the result of some artisan's skill, and noted that it had been exhibited at the Turf Coffee House in London for a fee of one shilling. The two-foot-long mini-monstrosity dropped out of sight soon after that when a former employer of Eades took legal action to demand a share of the exhibit. But thousands of Londoners paid

4   No need to worry about eyes; the nostrils will be in the correct position to pass for eye-sockets.

5   Pin the trimmed carcass to a block of wood, arranging and "sculpting" the parts imaginatively and allow it to dry in the sun. As it dries, the fin supports will shrivel into a resemblance of crossed arms.

6   When thoroughly dry, add a coat of varnish to seal the surface.

Figure 9.3   *A manufactured Jenny Haniver.* (Kimberly Poeppy-DelRio)

their shillings to have a look at the thing while it was still the talk of the town.[113]

It would not be the last of its kind, however, as a raft of similar frauds came out of what was apparently a new cottage industry in Japan. "The 'mermaids,'" says Richard Ellis, in *Monsters of the Sea*, ". . . usually consisted of cleverly conjoined skeletons of little monkeys and dehydrated fishes . . . and mermaids of all shapes and sizes became surprisingly popular."[114]

That master showman, P.T. Barnum, heard about Captain Eades's mermaid in 1842, 20 years after its London exhibition. After Eades died, his son sold it to the owner of a Boston collector of curiosities, who sold it to Barnum. Barnum claimed the mermaid had been captured in the Feejee (Fiji) Islands, preserved in China, and purchased by a London doctor. Due to Barnum's stupendous promotional skills, the shriveled conglomeration of animal parts now known as the **Feejee Mermaid** was a giant hit in New York City.

Years later, Barnum confessed his trickery in his autobiography. But his success inspired many imitators. Fake sea creatures and mermaids inexplicably came to be called **Jenny Hanivers**. And while these imitation merpeople will never explain the thousands of sightings of huge and unidentified sea creatures the world over, there is some satisfaction in being able to get a handle on at least a small part of the mystery, as Nessie and her big green cousins swim on.

Timeline

5000 BCE (circa)   Sculptures of the fish-god Oannes are made by Babylonians

3000 (circa)   Sea monster Labbu described in ancient Sumerian text, *The Sumerian Epic of Creation and Paradise*

1380–1360   Date of the Ugaritic myths, including the sea monster Yam

1000   Earliest written record of the word "kraken," found in a Norse manuscript

700   Homer's legends of Greek sea creatures such as the Triton and Scylla are written

200   The *Mahabarata*, ancient Hindu scripture of India with tales of giant serpent, is first recorded

558 CE   Northern Irish mermaid is claimed taken from Belfast Lough

750–1350   Scandinavian tales reveal Jormungand, the Midgard serpent that encircled the earth

1403   Mermaid is reported in Netherlands village

1639   A large, serpent-like creature is sighted off Cape Ann, Massachusetts

1600s, mid   Serpent-like lake monster sightings begin in Lake Storsjön, Sweden

1680   A kraken snags itself on rocks off the coast of Norway

1800s, early   Reported sightings of Mishiginabig, antlered sea serpent of Ojibwe lore, in the Great Lakes region of the Midwestern United States

1817 The Gloucester Serpent is sighted off Gloucester, Massachusetts

1822 The "Feejee Mermaid" is first exhibited by Captain Eades from Boston

1823 Hernando Grijalva sees a cavorting sea-ape off the coast of southern California

1836 Hans Christian Andersen writes "The Little Mermaid"

1842 The Feejee Mermaid is exhibited in New York City by P.T. Barnum

1848 A large, long-necked sea monster is seen by the crew of the H.M.S. *Daedaelus* off St. Helena in the South Atlantic

1855 Great monster hoax takes place on Silver Lake in northwestern New York

1857 Johan Steenstrup publishes a scientific paper on the giant squid, naming it *Architeuthis*

1873 Champ, monster of Lake Champlain, New York, is said to have a collision with a boat

1880 A 65-foot-long giant squid is found on a beach in Newfoundland

1890 Steamer captain sees serpentine creature (Ogopogo) in Okanagan Lake, British Columbia

1800s, late Danish sailing ship encounters a kraken or giant squid off West African coast

1902 Serpent-like creature is seen in Geneva Lake in southern Wisconsin

1905 Three members of the British Zoological Society on the yacht *Valhalla* see a long-necked sea monster near Key West, Florida

1913 German captain first reports the Mokele-m'bembe, thought to be a living dinosaur, in Cameroon and the Congo

1914 Eel or snakelike creature is seen in Lough Abisdealy, Ireland

1930s, mid A green-haired mermaid is spotted off the coast of Africa's Cape Horn

1933   A flurry of sightings are widely reported of Nessie, the Loch Ness Monster in a Scotland lake

1936   Chessie is first spotted in Chesapeake Bay, off Maryland

1968   First movie film of Ogopogo is captured on Okanagan Lake, British Columbia

1977   Japanese trawler off New Zealand takes remains of what is first claimed to be a plesiosaur but turns out to be a decomposed basking shark

1978   Four reptilian creatures are seen in Chesapeake Bay by a former CIA agent

1980   Video made of Ogopogo by Larry Thal in Okanagan Lake, British Columbia

1980   James Powell and Roy P. Mackal travel to the Congo and interview eyewitnesses of Mokele m'bembe

1980   25 witnesses in charter boats see Chessie in Chesapeake Bay

1982   Smithsonian scientific panel examines a video of the Chesapeake Bay creature, Chessie

1985   Serpentine creature is seen in Lake Storsjön, Sweden, by a family of five

1988   Japanese team sees unidentified water creature in Lake Tele, the Congo

1988   Lizard man chases a teen in a car in Bishopville, South Carolina

1989   Video made of Ogopogo by Ken Chaplin on Okanagan Lake, British Columbia

1980s, late   Genny the lake monster is seen by two teens in the Ohio River, Kentucky

1993   Lizard man surprises a man and his son on a riverbank in LaCrosse, Wisconsin

1995   Latest reported sighting of Chessie in Chesapeake Bay

1990s, mid   B.M. Nunnelly sees the head and neck of an unknown creature in the Ohio River, Kentucky

2001   Large, snakelike creature is seen in the Geneva area of Kentucky

2005   An amphibious man is seen paddling in the Caspian Sea not far from Iran

2005   Fossil of the fishapod, prehistoric transitional creature, is found in Canada

2006   ABC News obtains a video of the creature known as Champ in Lake Champlain, New York

2007   A 26-foot-long giant squid is found on a beach off southern Australia

2007   A 33-foot-long Colossal Squid is taken off New Zealand

2007   50,000 cameras are handed out to attendees of the "Rock Ness" concert in Scotland in an attempt to capture photos of Nessie, the water creature of Loch Ness

Glossary

ABYSSOPELAGIC ZONE Deep region of the ocean 13,000–20,000 below the surface

ANANTA SHESHA Giant, 100-headed sea serpent of Hindu origin

APEP Giant, primeval serpent-god of Egypt

APOPHIS Greek name for Apep

AQUATIC CREATURES Beings that live in water

ARCHETYPE Subconscious mental symbol common to all humans

ARCHITEUTHIS Scientific name for the giant squid

BARYONYX An extinct, alligator-snouted aquatic reptile

BASILOSAURUS Original Latin name for a toothed whale later named the *Zeuglodon*

BOBO An elephant-like sea monster that has appeared regularly in modern times off Monterey, California

BUNYIP An Australian water monster of varying descriptions

CEPHALOPODS Class of creatures including the octopus and squid, literally means "head-foot"

CHAMP Monster of Lake Champlain, New York

CHESSIE Sea monster said to live in Chesapeake Bay between Virginia and Maryland

CHIMERAS Fantastic beings with parts from several different beasts

CLASSIC SEA SERPENT Classification of sea monsters that includes large, serpentine creatures

CRYPTIDS "Hidden" animals, or ones unknown to orthodox science

DAGON   Merman-god worshipped by the Philistines in Old Testament times

DEVIL-DEVIL   Australian Aboriginal snakelike lake creature

DIPROTODON   An extinct marsupial the size of a hippo but related to the wombat, thought by some to be the origin of Australian bunyip legends

DRACONTOLOGY   The study and investigation of unknown aquatic animals

DRAGON KING   Aquatic dragon said to rule all Japanese lakes

FEEJEE MERMAID   An assemblage of ape and fish carcasses exhibited as a mermaid in London and New York in the first half of the 1800s

FISHAPOD   Nine-foot creature from the Devonian period which had characteristics of both land and sea animals

GENNY   Monster seen in the Ohio River, Kentucky, in the late 1980s

GLOBSTERS   Remains of partially decayed sea creatures such as basking sharks, jellyfish, octopuses, or whales that wash up on beaches and are presumed to be sea monster carcasses

HADAL ZONE   Deepest trench areas of the ocean reaching 20,000 to 36,200 feet below the surface

ICHTHYOSAUR   Prehistoric seagoing reptile with a long, sharp beak, and eel or dolphin-shaped body

JENNY   Serpent-like creature seen in Geneva Lake in southern Wisconsin around the turn of the nineteenth and twentieth centuries

JENNY HANIVERS   Fake mermaids or other mystery creatures made by disfiguring and/or joining parts of animals

JORMUNGAND   Ancient mythic Norse sea monster believed long enough to encircle the world, also known as the Midgard Monster

KAI KWAI   Round-eyed "Sea Devil" of Hong Kong

KAPPA   A Japanese, monkey-like water spirit

KELPIE   Shape-shifting legendary creature of Scotland that took the form of a horse to lure travelers into the water, also called a water horse

KRAKEN   Norse term for a sea monster resembling a giant squid

LABBU   Mythic river monster of Mesopotamia

LEVIATHAN   Gigantic sea monster described in the Bible's Old Testament, with crocodile and serpentine features

LOCH   Scottish word meaning a land-locked waterway or lake

MARSUPIAL   An animal that bears live young at such an immature stage that they must be nurtured in a pouch until sufficient growth is obtained

MEMPHRE   Dragon-headed creature of Lake Memphremagog, between Canada and Vermont

MISHI GINABIG   North American Algonquin antlered sea serpent believed to inhabit the Great Lakes

MISHIPESHU (OR MICHI-PICHOUX)   A fearsome water lynx believed by many North American Algonquin tribes to inhabit waterways; often blamed for stirring up dangerous rapids and for human abductions, and usually represented with horns and a long, whip-like tail, and sometimes a snakelike body

MOKELE M'BEMBE   African water creature seen in contemporary times and believed to be a relict species of dinosaur

MO'OO   Hawaiian shiny, black, 30-foot-long creature that inhabits fish ponds

MOSASAURUS   Prehistoric marine reptile with a tubular body and alligator-like snout

NAGAS   Snakelike, partly human, divine beings of India

NAIADS   Greek water nymphs, creatures that resembled beautiful women, known for luring men into the sea

NESSIE   Lake monster alleged to live in Loch Ness, Scotland, since the 500s CE

N'HA-A-ITK   Native American name for Okanagan Lake creature in British Columbia; later named Ogopogo

OANNES   Babylonian fish-god and teacher of mankind

OGOPOGO   Serpent-like monster of Okanagan Lake in southern British Columbia

OLD MAN OF THE SEA   A serpent-like creature that has appeared regularly off the coast of Monterey Bay, California, in modern times

PEAT   Partly decayed plant materials, the basis of coal

PHOTOPHORES   Circular, bioluminescent organs found on deep-sea creatures

PINNIPEDS   Animal order including the seal family

RELICTS   Creatures of a species thought to be extinct that has in fact survived

RONGO MAI   Polynesian god of whales

SCYLLA   Six-headed sea nymph-turned-monster that lived in a narrow sea channel

SEICHE   A moving wave of water elevated above the surface so that it seems to be "standing"

SIRENS   Birdlike creatures of Greek mythology that later evolved into lovely sea maidens

STORSJOODJURET   Lake monster seen in Lake Storsjön, Sweden, since mid-1600s

TANGAROA   Polynesian sea god, creator of humanity

TRITON   Ancient Greek merman, half fish and half man

TYLOSAURUS   Ancient marine reptile of the mosasaur family

UNKTEHI   North American Plains tribe water monster that looks like an oversized cow

UNKTEHILA   Cherokee snakelike water monster

VAMPIRE SQUID   Species of tiny squid with rows of sharp, toothlike spikes along its arms

WATER HORSES   Types of sea monsters with a long neck, small head, lumpy body, and flipper-like appendages

WOLF EEL   Large, toothed eellike creature of the North Atlantic

YAM   An ancient Syrian sea god in serpent form

ZEUGLODON   An ancient, toothed whale thought to be extinct

Endnotes

1. Ulrich Magin, "Something Fishy," *Strange Magazine* #10, Fall-Winter 1992.

2. Sam D. Gill and Irene Sullivan, *Dictionary of Native American Mythology* (New York: Oxford University Press, 1992), 189.

3. "2006 is Banner Year for Discoveries of New Species in Borneo's Rainforests," *Science Daily*. Available online. URL: http://www.sciencedaily.com/releases/2006/12/061219095311.htm (accessed January 8, 2008).

4. Roger Payne and Genevieve Johnson, "Andrew's Beaked Whales," PBS – The Voyage of the Odyssey – Track the Voyage – Australia. Available online. URL: http://www.pbs.org/odyssey/odyssey/20020424_log_transcript.html (accessed January 8, 2008).

5. David D. Gilmore, *Monsters: Evil Beings, Mythical Beasts, and All Manner of Imaginary Terrors* (Philadelphia: University of Pennsylvania Press, 2003).

6. Stephen L. Caiger, "The Early Chapters of Genesis," Bible and Spade, Ch. 2. Katapi Bible Resource Pages. Available online. URL: http://www.katapi.org.uk. First published Oxford, UK: Oxford University Press, 1936 (accessed January 8, 2008).

7. Arthur Cotterell and Rachel Storm, *The Ultimate Encyclopedia of Mythology* (London: Hermes House, 2006), 329.

8. Gilmore, 33.

9. Ibid., 34.

10. Wallis E. Budge, *Egyptian Magic* (New York: Citadel Press, 1991), 80.

11. "Apophis," The Stargate Omnipedia. Available online. URL: http://www.gateworld.net/omnipedia/characters/links/apophis.shtml (downloaded on June 27, 2007).

12. The Bhagavad-Gita: Questions and Answers. Available online. URL: http://www.bhagavad-gita.org/Articles/faq.html (accessed March 30, 2008).

13. Paul Harrison, *Sea Serpents and Lake Monsters of the British Isles* (London: Robert Hale, Ltd., 2001), 12.

14. Linda S. Godfrey, *The Beast of Bray Road: Tailing Wisconsin's Werewolf* (Madison, Wisc.: Prairie Oak Press, 2003), 61.

15. Sam D. Gill and Irene F. Sullivan, *Dictionary of Native American*

Mythology (New York: Oxford University Press, 1992), 321.

16. Virginia Morell, "Beyond Nessie," *National Geographic*. Available online. URL: http://ngm.nationalgeographic.com/ngm/0512/feature3/index.html (posted December 2005).

17. David D. Gilmore, *Monsters: Evil Beings, Mythical Beasts, and All Manner of Imaginary Terrors* (Philadelphia: University of Pennsylvania Press, 2003), 2.

18. John Keel, *The Complete Guide to Mysterious Beings* (New York: Tor Books, 2002), 284.

19. Jan Knappert, *Pacific Mythology: An Encyclopedia of Myth and Legend* (London: Diamond Books, 1995), 149.

20. Cleo Whittaker (contributing editor), *An Introduction to Oriental Mythology* (Secaucus, N.J.: Quintent Books, 1989), 112–113.

21. Knappert, 65–66.

22. Gilmore, 149–150.

23. Ronan Coghlan, *A Dictionary of Cryptozoology* (Bangor, Northern Ireland: Xiphos Books, 2004), 43–44.

24. Ibid., 44.

25. Neil Arnold, *Alien Zoo: the A-Z of Zooform Phenomena* (Bideford, U.K.: Crypto-a-go-go, 2005), 35.

26. Roy Mackal, *Searching for Hidden Animals; an Inquiry into Zoological Mysteries* (Garden City, N.Y.: Doubleday & Company, 1980), 65.

27. William Gibbons, "Was a Mokele-mbembe Killed at Lake Tele?" The Anomalist, Archive, High Strangeness Report. Available

online. URL: http://www.anomalist.com/reports/mokele.html (downloaded July 18, 2007).

28. Ibid.

29. Linda Godfrey, *Weird Michigan; Your Travel Guide to Michigan's Local Legends and Best Kept Secrets* (New York: Sterling Publishing Co., 2006), 28–29.

30. Richard Ellis, *Monsters of the Sea* (New York: Alfred Knopf, 1996), 77.

31. "Berossus on Creation," Livius: Articles on Human History. Available online. URL: http://www.livius.org/be-bm/berossus/berossus-q01.html (downloaded July 18, 2007).

32. Arthur Cotterell and Rachel Storm, *The Ultimate Encyclopedia of Mythology* (London: Hermes House, 2006), 274.

33. Thomas Flaherty, editor, *Mysterious Creatures* (*Mysteries of the Unknown*) (Richmond, Va.: Time Life Books, 1991), 54.

34. "Tritones," Theoi Project: Guide to Greek Mythology. Available online. URL: http://www.theoi.com/Pontios/Tritones.html (downloaded July 19, 2007).

35. Reader's Digest Assn., Inc., *Strange Stories; Amazing Facts* (Pleasantville, N.Y.: Reader's Digest Assn., 1976), 423.

36. Reader's Digest Assn., 418–419.

37. Ibid., 418-419.

38. Loren Coleman, "California Sea-Ape?" Cryptomundo. Available online. URL: http://www.cryptomundo.com/cryptozoo-news/ca-sea-ape/ (accessed January 8, 2008).

39. Ibid.

40. Ulrich Magin, "Something Fishy," *Strange Magazine*, #10, Fall-Winter 1992.

41. Ibid.

42. Karl Shuker, "Saga of the St. Helena Sirenians," *Strange Magazine*, #11, Spring-Summer 1993.

43. M.A. Drimmer, editor, "Manatees – Too Peaceable for Their Own Good," in *The Illustrated Encyclopedia of Animal Life*, *Vol. 6* (New York: Greystone Press, 1961), 625.

44. Linda S. Godfrey, *Hunting the American Werewolf* (Madison, Wisc.: Trails Books, 2006), 241.

45. Ibid., 248.

46. Joseph Trainor, editor, "Aquaman Spotted in the Caspian Sea," *UFO Roundup*. Available online. URL: http://www.ufoinfo.com/roundup/v10/rnd1018.shtml (downloaded July 24, 2007).

47. James B. Sweeney, *Sea Monsters; A Collection of Eyewitness Accounts* (New York: David McKay Co., 1977), 63.

48. James B. Sweeney, *A Pictorial History of Sea Monsters and Other Dangerous Marine Life* (New York: Crown Publishers, 1972), 73–78.

49. A.C. Oudemans, *The Great Sea-Serpent* (Landisville, Penn.: Coachwhip Publications, 2007), 134.

50. "Chessie," Maryland Department of Natural Resources Information Resource Center. Available online. URL: http://www.dnr.state.md.us/irc/chessie/history.html (downloaded July 25, 2007).

51. Loren Coleman and Patrick Huyghe, *The Field Guide to Lake Monsters, Sea Serpents, and Other Mystery Denizens of the Deep* (New York: Penguin Group, 2003), 66–68.

52. M.A. Frizzell, "'Chessie' (the Chesapeake Bay Phenomenon)," UMBC: An Honor University in Maryland. Available online. URL: http://www.research.umbc.edu/~frizzell /chessie.html (Accessed January 8, 2008).

53. "Chessie," Maryland Department of Natural Resources Information Resource Center. Available online. URL: http://www.dnr.state.md.us/irc/chessie/history.html (downloaded July 25, 2007).

54. Ibid.

55. James B. Sweeney, *Sea Monsters; A Collection of Eyewitness Accounts* (New York: David McKay Co., 1977), 67–69.

56. Ibid., 68.

57. Ibid., 69.

58. Randall A. Reinstedt, *Shipwrecks and Sea Monsters of California's Central Coast* (Carmel, Calif.: Ghost Town Publications, 1975), 149.

59. "Heuvelmans Sea Monster Classifications." SCIFIPEDIA. Available Online. URL: http://scifipedia.scifi.com/index.php/Heuvelmans_Sea_Monster_Classifications (downloaded July 27, 2007).

60. Roy P. Mackal, *Searching for Hidden Animals: An Inquiry into Zoological Mysteries* (Garden City, N.Y.: Doubleday & Co., Inc., 1980), 19.

61. Coleman and Huyghe, 36.

62. Ibid., 42.

63. Ibid., 44.

64. Ibid., 147.

65. Ibid.,157.

66. Joseph J. Thorndike, Jr., editor, *Mysteries of the Deep* (New York: American Heritage Publishing Co., 1980), 281.

67. James B. Sweeney, *A Pictorial History of Sea Monsters and Other Dangerous Marine Life* (New York: Crown Publishers, 1972), 31.

68. Angus Hall, *Monsters and Mythic Beasts* (Garden City, N.Y.: Doubleday and Company, Inc., 1976), 51.

69. Steve O'Shea, "Giant Squid and Colossal Squid Fact Sheet," The Octopus News Magazine Online. Available online. URL: http://www.tonmo.com/science/public/giantsq uidfacts.php (downloaded August 2, 2007).

70. Associated Press, "As Big as a Bus; Dead Squid Washes Up in Australia," *The Milwaukee Journal Sentinel*, July 12, 2007.

71. Paul Rogers, "Giant Squid Take Liking to California," *The Milwaukee Journal Sentinel*, July 30, 2007.

72. David Scheel, "Giant Octopus Fact Sheet." The Giant Octopus Web Page. Available online. URL: http://marine.alaskapacific.edu/octopus/factsheet.html (accessed January 8, 2008).

73. Nunnelly, B.M. *Mysterious Kentucky: The History, Mystery and Unexplained of the Bluegrass State.* Decatur, Ill.: Whitechapel Press, 2007, 27.

74. Coleman and Huyghe, 251.

75. Linda S. Godfrey, *Strange Wisconsin: More Badger State Weirdness* (Madison, Wisc.: Trails Books, 2007), 56–57.

76. Paul B. Jenkins, *History and Indian Remains of Lake Geneva and Lake Como* (Lake Geneva, Wisc.: Privately published).

77. Peter Costello, "Lake Monsters of the New World," in *Mysteries of Space and Time: the Unexplained, Vol. 1* (Westport, Conn.: H.S. Stuttman, Inc., 1992), 94, 100–101.

78. Lee Paul, "Ogopogo," The Unexplained. Available online. URL: http://www.theoutlaws.com/unexplained7.htm (downloaded August 7, 2007).

79. Adam Sisman, *The World's Most Incredible Stories: the Best of Fortean Times* (London, U.K.: Eddison Sadd Editions and Barnes & Noble, 1998), 44.

80. Karl P.N. Shuker, "Lesser-Known Lake Monsters," *FATE*. September 1990.

81. Ibid., 76.

82. Paul Harrison, *Sea Serpents and Lake Monsters of the British Isles* (London: Robert Hale Ltd., 2001), 209.

83. Coleman and Huyghe, 49, 72.

84. Robert D. San Souci, *The Loch Ness Monster: Great Mysteries, Opposing Viewpoints.* Minneapolis: Greenhaven Press, 1989).

85. David Wallechinsky and Irving Wallace, "History of the Search for the Loch Ness Monster Part 1," Trivia-Library.com. Available online. URL: http://www.trivia-

library.com/b/history-of-the-search-for-the-loch-ness-monster-part-1.htm (downloaded June 6, 2007).

86. Tony Harmsworth, "Loch Ness Monster Eyewitness Accounts," Tony Harmsworth's Loch Ness Information Web site. Available online. URL: http://www.loch-ness.org/eyewitnesses.html (downloaded June 4, 2007).

87. W.H. Grattan-Flood, "Saint Adamnan," New Advent. Available online. URL: http:// www.newadvent.org/cathen/01135c.htm (downloaded June 7, 2007).

88. Richard Forrest, "A Few Reasons Why the Loch Ness Monster is not a Plesiosaur," The Plesiosaur Site. Available online. URL: http://www.plesiosaur.com/lochness.php (downloaded June 11, 2007).

89. Angus Hall, *Monsters and Mythic Beasts* (Garden City, N.Y.: Double-day and Company, 1976), 72.

90. Ibid., 73.

91. Ibid., 74.

92. "The Beast of Loch Ness: Birth of a Legend, Part Three," Nova Online. Available online. URL: http://www.pbs.org/wgbh/nova/lochness/legend3.html (accessed January 8, 2008).

93. Richard Forrest, "Five Questions," The Plesiosaur Site. Available online. URL: http://www.plesiosaur.com/five.questions/five.questions.php (downloaded June 11, 2007).

94. "Loch Ness 'Monster,'" The Skeptic's Dictionary. Available online. URL: http://www.skepdic.com/nessie.html (accessed January 8, 2008).

95. Richard Ellis, "Terrible Lizards of the Sea," *Natural History*, September 2003.

96. Coleman and Huyghe, 49.

97. David Eldridge, *Sea Monsters* (Mahwah, N.J.: Troll Associates, 1980), 31.

98. Richard Ellis, "Terrible Lizards of the Sea," *Natural History*, September 2003.

99. Douglas Dixon, *The Illustrated Dinosaur Encyclopedia* (New York: Gallery Books, 1988), 80–81.

100. Roy P. Mackal, *Searching for Hidden Animals* (Garden City, N.Y.: Doubleday and Co., 1980), 21.

101. A.C. Oudemans, *The Great Sea Serpent* (Landisville, Penn.: Coachwhip Publications, 2007 (first published 1892)), 329.

102. Stefan Lovgren, "Godzilla Fossils Reveal Real-Life Sea Monster," *National Geographic News*. Available online. URL: http://news.nationalgeographic.com/news/2005/11/1110_051110_sea_monster.html (accessed January 8, 2008).

103. Madeleine J. Nash, "Our Cousin the Fishapod," *Time*, April 17, 2006, 167, no. 16.

104. Glen J. Kuban, "Sea Monster or Shark: An Analysis of a Supposed Plesiosaur Carcass Netted in 1977," originally published in *Reports of the National Center for Science Education*, May/June 1997, 17, no. 3, 16–28. Kuban's Websites. Available online. URL: http://paleo.cc/paluxy/plesios.htm (downloaded on May 30, 2007).

105. Linda Godfrey, *The Beast of Bray Road: Tailing Wisconsin's Werewolf* (Madison, Wisc.: Trails Books, 2003), 160.

106. Peter Doyle, "My Battle with Giant Eel 100-Feet Under Sea" *Daily Record*. Available online. URL: http://www.dailyrecord. co.uk.news/tmobjectid=1443119 4&method=full&siteid=89488& headline=my-battle-with-giant-eel-100ft-under-sea-name_page. html. Posted July 16, 2004.

107. Oudemans, 287.

108. Ibid., 360–361.

109. Coleman and Huyghe, 86–87.

110. Oudemans, 422.

111. John Keel, *The Complete Guide to Mysterious Beings* (New York: Tor Books, 2002), 300–302.

112. Ibid., 84.

113. C.J.S. Thompson, *The Mystery and Lore of Monsters* (New Hyde Park, N.Y.: University Books, 1968), 111–115.

114. Richard Gillis, *Monsters of the Sea* (New York: Alfred A. Knopf, 1996), 81.

Further Resources

WEB SITES

Cryptomundo
http://www.cryptomundo.com
Devoted to all types of cryptid (unknown or hidden) creatures, Cryptomundo contains archives of new stories dealing with all kinds of water monsters, and is a place to check daily for news breaks dealing with Loch Ness and other sea and lake creature developments.

The Octopus News Magazine Online
http://www.tonmo.com/science/public/giantsquidfacts.php
All you ever wanted to know about giant squid and octopods, with fact sheets and illustrations.

The Plesiosaur Site
http://www.plesiosaur.com/five.questions/five.questions.php
This site presents a thorough and scientific look at plesiosaurs, prehistoric creatures most often cited as a possible explanation for sea and lake monsters.

Tony Harmsworth's Loch Ness Information Web site
http://www.loch-ness.org/eyewitnesses.html
Learn everything about Nessie, from eyewitness accounts to the history and geography of the Loch Ness area. Highly organized, and includes illustrations.

BOOKS

Coleman, Loren, and Patrick Huyghe. *The Field Guide to Lake Monsters, Sea Serpents, and Other Mystery Denizens of the Deep.* New York: Penguin, 2003.

Coleman and Huyghe have organized sea and lake monsters into 14 different types, with illustrations and supporting accounts for each one, and fascinating historical tidbits interwoven throughout the text.

Cotterell, Arthur and Rachel Storm. *The Ultimate Encyclopedia of Mythology.* London: Anness Publishing, 2006.

A very large coffee table–style book featuring a lavishly illustrated cache of world water monster lore from various ancient civilizations, including insightful sidebars.

Gilmore, David G. *Monsters, Evil Beings, Mythical Beasts, and All Manner of Imaginary Terrors.* Philadelphia: University of Pennsylvania Press, 2003.

A great historical overview of both well-known monsters and more obscure creatures, Gilmore's *Monsters* includes a deep pool of sea and lake beasts, observed and mythic.

Sweeney, James B. *A Pictorial History of Sea Monsters and Other Dangerous Marine Life.* New York: Crown Publishers, 1972.

This is an older book but its oversized pages contain one of the best collections of monster accounts and historical art anywhere.

Thorndike, Joseph J., editor. *Mysteries of the Deep.* New York: Charles Scribner's Sons, 1980.

In-depth articles on not only sea monsters but all aspects of the world's seas, the plants and animals that live there, and man's constant quest to learn the secrets of the oceans.

GAMES

Sea Monsters: A Prehistoric Adventure (2007). Destination Software for Playstation 2.

Discover strange creatures under the sea in six unique underwater zones, as either the hunter or the hunted in this action/adventure game.

VIDEOS

Chased by Sea Monsters, a 2004 Discovery Channel show available on DVD.

In this 100-minute video, zoologist Nigel Marven scours seven prehistoric seas for creatures like the giant Megalodon shark. Computer animations are breathtakingly realistic.

The Beast of Loch Ness, a 2006 *Nova* release available on DVD.

Investigators Bob Rines and Charlie Wyckoff make a trip to Loch Ness for Nova in hopes of finding Nessie with the latest in sonar technology. The film explores the Loch Ness history and terrain, and examines old photos with new techniques.

The Living Sea, IMAX, a 1995 2-Disc WMVHD Edition.

Watch a star-studded tour of exotic underwater locals that give a great feel for the strangeness of known sea creatures. The two disks, with a running total of 77 minutes, take viewers on a worldwide excursion to swim with humpback whales and watch cuttlefish change colors, among other undersea wonders.

Index

About the Author

LINDA S. GODFREY worked as a newspaper reporter and columnist for *The Week*, a county newspaper published in Delavan, Wisconsin, for 10 years. She won National Newspaper Association first-place awards for feature stories in 1996, 1998, and 2000. She is the author of *The Beast of Bray Road* and *Hunting the American Werewolf*, as well as two volumes in the Barnes & Noble "Weird" series: *Weird Wisconsin* (co-authored with Richard D. Hendricks), *Weird Michigan*, and *Strange Wisconsin*. She has appeared on many national television and radio programs as an expert on anomalous creatures, including *Inside Edition*, Animal Planet Channel, *The New In Search Of* (SCI FI Channel), Travel Channel, Discovery Kids, *Northern Mysteries* on Canada's Global Network, and the *Jeff Rense, Clyde Lewis, Rob McConnell*, and *Coast to Coast AM* radio shows. She is also an illustrator and artist, and she maintains a Web site on werewolf sightings and news at http://www.beastofbrayroad.com. She lives with her husband, Steven, in rural southeastern Wisconsin.

About the Consulting Editor

ROSEMARY ELLEN GUILEY is one of the foremost authorities on the paranormal. Psychic experiences in childhood led to her lifelong study and research of paranormal mysteries. A journalist by training, she has worked full time in the paranormal since 1983, as an author, presenter, and investigator. She has written 31 nonfiction books on paranormal topics, translated into 13 languages, and hundreds of articles. She has experienced many of the phenomena she has researched. She has appeared on numerous television, documentary, and radio shows. She is also a member of the League of Paranormal Gentlemen for Spooked Productions, a columnist for *TAPS Paramagazine*, a consulting editor for *FATE* magazine, and writer for the "Paranormal Insider" blog. Ms. Guiley's books include *The Encyclopedia of Angels*, *The Encyclopedia of Magic and Alchemy*, *The Encyclopedia of Saints*, *The Encyclopedia of Vampires, Werewolves, and Other Monsters*, and *The Encyclopedia of Witches and Witchcraft*, all from Facts On File. She lives in Maryland and her Web site is http://www.visionaryliving.com.